A. CONNORS	FIONA BARKER	MICHELLE COOK
ABI DARÉ	GEMMA FOWLER	MIKE GOULD
ALEX MULLARKY	GILL LEWIS	MIMI THEBO
ALISON LAYLAND	GUINEVERE GLASFURD	MITCH JOHNSON
AMY LILWALL	HANNAH GOLD	MOIRA MCPARTLIN
ANGELA KECOJEVIC	HARRY WHITEHEAD	N R BAKER
ANNA M HOLMES	IAN MCDONALD	N.E. MCMORRAN
ANNA MCKERROW	ISABEL THOMAS	NICK WOOD
ANNE CHARNOCK	J J GREEN	NICOLA PENFOLD
ANNEMARIE ALLAN	JAMIE MOLLART	NICKY SINGER
ANTHEA SIMMONS	JANE ROGERS	PAUL GOODENOUGH
ANTONIA MAXWELL	JAY ASPEN	PAUL MCAULEY
APRIL DOYLE	JEREMY BROWN	PHIL GILVIN
BILL MCGUIRE	JIM PEARCE	PIERS TORDAY
BRIANNA CRAFT	JOAN HAIG	RAB FERGUSON
BROGEN MURPHY	JOANNE O'CONNELL	RAY STAR
CAOILINN HUGHES	JOHN IRONMONGER	RB KELLY
CARYS BRAY	JOSH LACEY	ROZ DINEEN
CHARLOTTE R. MENDEL	JOSH MARTIN	RUTH HARTLEY
CHITRA SOUNDAR	JULIE BERTAGNA	S J MORDEN
CHRIS BECKETT	KATE KELLY	SARAH BLAKE
CLARE REES	KENECHI UDOGU	SARAH CROSSAN
CHRIS VICK	KEVAN MANWARING	SARAH HOLDING
D.A. BADEN	LAURA BAGGALEY	STEPHANIE BURGIS
DAVID BARKER	LAURA WOOD	SUNITI NAMJOSHI
DAVID THORPE	LAUREN ST JOHN	TOLÁ OKOGWU
DEBORAH TOMKINS	LINDA NEWBERY	TOM HUDDLESTON
E L LAM	LYNDSEY CROAL	VASHTI HARDY
ELE FOUNTAIN	LIZZIE PEPPER	VENETIA WELBY
EMMA GEEN	LYNN BUCKLE	VICKI JARRETT
EMMA REYNOLDS	M. G. LEONARD	WILLIAM SUTCLIFFE
EMMA SHEVAH	MANDA SCOTT	YABA BADOE
EMILY BUCHANAN	MARIAN WOMACK	ZILLAH BETHELL
FARAH ALI	MARK BALLABON	

WREN JAMES (FOUNDER)

LEAGUE MEMBERS
IN US & CANADA

ABHI SUKHDIAL
A.E. COPENHAVER
AARON J ARSENAULT
AHUVA BATYA SCHARFF
ALLISTER THOMPSON
ANDREW DANA HUDSON
ANDREW DOLBERG
ANGIE HOCKMAN
ANNA BURKE
ARIC MCBAY
ASHLEY SELBY
AUSTIN ASLAN
AYA DE LEÓN
BRIGHTFLAME
BRUCE SMITH
C.S. MACCATH
CARA HOFFMAN
CARRIE FIRESTONE
CATHERINE BUSH
CHARLIE JANE ANDERS
CLAIRE DATNOW
CLAIRE HOLROYDE
CLARA HUME
CLARA WARD
CLYDE BOYER
CORY DOCTOROW
CRAIG RUSSELL
CYNTHIA ZHANG
DEBBIE URBANSKI
DEENA METZGER

DENISE S. ROBBINS
DIANE OWENS PRETTYMAN
DIANE TURNSHEK
DONNA GLEE WILLIAMS
D. G. DRIVER
EDAN LEPUCKI
EMILY GRANDY
FELICITY HARLEY
FRANCESCA VARELA
FREDERICK TURNER
GEORGINA KEY
JANNA MCMAHAN
JOAN HE
JOEL BURCAT
JOHN YUNKER
JULIE DALTON
KATE RISSE
KATE WOODWORTH
KATY YOCOM
KARL SCHROEDER
KRITIKA H. RAO
LAUREN C. TEFFEAU
LILY BROOKS-DALTON
LYDIA MILLET
MARISSA SLAVEN
MARJORIE B. KELLOGG
MARK S. JOHNSON
MARY FLODIN
MARYANN LESERT
MAXINE KAPLAN
MICHAEL J. DELUCA

MIDGE RAYMOND
MONICA SHERWOOD
NIKKI KALLIO
NINA MUNTEANU
PAUL DALTON
P J HOOVER
P. FINIAN REILLY
PAOLO BACIGALUPI
RACHEL GRIFFIN
REBECCA ROANHORSE
ROB LONG
S W LAWRENCE
SAM J MILLER
SAMANTHA M CLARK
SARA ST. ANTOINE
SARAH E. LEWIS
SARENA ULIBARRI
SAUL TANPEPPER
SENA DESAI GOPAL
SEQUOIA NAGAMATSU
SHARON J. WISHNOW
SIM KERN
STEPHANIE BECKER
STEVE TOMASULA
STEVEN L. PECK
SUSAN FLETCHER
TIM CHAWAGA
TOBIAS BUCKELL
TRACY RICHARDSON
VANESSA SAUNDERS

THE
CLIMATE-
CONSCIOUS
WRITERS
HANDBOOK

Created by the
Climate Fiction Writers League,
with support from **Climate Spring**
climate-fiction.org

Are you a writer who's worried about the environment? Would you like to learn how to weave climate themes into genres like romance, thrillers or literary fiction? This journal is for you!

This playful, interactive handbook is designed to support you through every stage in the writing process - from first idea to drafting and querying.

It was created for all kinds of writers who want to talk about climate change. It will demystify the process, build confidence and help us to journey collaboratively together.

You have permission to write about the climate crisis. You don't need expertise in science. You don't need to consider yourself an activist. You only need to be creative and imaginative.

NAME:

_____

◆ CONTACT DETAILS: ◆

_____

_____

_____

A BODY OF
WRITERS
WORKING FOR A
COMMON CAUSE
✦ CANNOT FAIL TO ✦
INFLUENCE
PUBLIC OPINION.

WOMEN WRITERS SUFFRAGE LEAGUE, 1908

The Climate Fiction Writers League is a group of authors who believe in the necessity of climate action, immediately and absolutely.

Fiction is one of the best ways to inspire passion, empathy and action in readers.

Our works:
- raise awareness of the climate emergency
- highlight solutions
- encourage action at the individual, corporate & government levels

This journal is designed to help writers create works that meet these goals. It was developed collaboratively with some of the world's foremost climate storytelling leaders, based on years of research and experience.

REWILD FOR VICTORY

Rewriting EXTINCTION

Comic by Maggie Behling
rewriting.earth

LEAGUE MEMBERS IN AUSTRALIA & NZ

BREN MACDIBBLE
CAROL GARDEN
DANIELLE CELERMAJER
DONNA M CAMERON
JAMES BRADLEY
JENNIFER MILLS
LINDA WOODROW
MICHAEL MUNTISOV
MARK SMITH
OCTAVIA CADE
REM WIGMORE

LEAGUE MEMBERS INTERNATIONALLY

ANA FILOMENA AMARAL (PORTUGAL)
ANJA STÜRZER (FRANCE)
HARRIET SPRINGBETT (FRANCE)
CHIOMA OKEREKE (FRANCE)
EMMI ITÄRANTA (FINLAND)
MARCUS SEDGWICK (SWITZERLAND)
JANE EKSTAM (SWEDEN)
JEAN-MARC LIGNY (GERMANY)
LIZ JENSEN (GERMANY)
UWE LAUB (DENMARK)

CLAUDIA ABOAF (ARGENTINA)
RENAN BERNARDO (BRAZIL)

QIUFAN CHEN (CHINA)
KHOA LE (VIETNAM)
STEVE WILLIS (MALAYSIA)
JAN LEE (HONG KONG)
NABEEL ISMEER (SINGAPORE)
STEVE STINE (SINGAPORE)
CRISTINA JURADO (UAE)

BIJAL VACHHARAJANI (INDIA)
SHALINI SRINIVASAN (INDIA)
RAJAT CHAUDHURI (INDIA)

Explore our members' climate fiction at <u>climate-fiction.org</u>

Climate storytelling is an exciting, expansive, broad and fast-growing area of writing. It is not a single genre, but a theme emerging across all types of fiction.

Climate fiction doesn't have to focus on communicating 'climate issues'. It can simply reflect the reality of our changing world. The best climate fiction strikes a balance between alarming realities and inspiring possibilities.

Climate fiction can...

- show characters' emotional, interior worlds, as they grow up in a changing climate.

- explore a sense of the uncanny, as the seasons and weather rapidly shift away from predictable cycles.

- highlight resilience and community in the face of disaster and difficulty.

- show the transition away from the polluting, extractive ways of being, to the joys of new ways of living within the world.

- discuss colonisation and the intersection of class, social inequality, racism and climate.

Climate fiction can...

- be humorous, light-hearted, fantastical and irreverent.

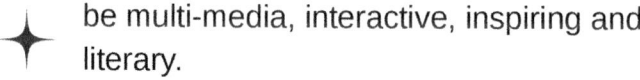
- be multi-media, interactive, inspiring and literary.

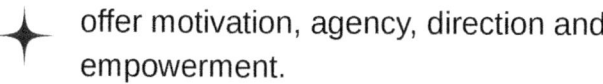
- offer motivation, agency, direction and empowerment.

- lead us towards a future where people and planet flourish together.

You have permission to write a story about the climate crisis. You don't need expertise in science. You don't need to consider yourself an activist. You only need to be creative and imaginative.

The following pages will help you to tell personal stories that connect with people and show them how they can make a difference. Use these prompts and resources as a springboard for your creativity. We don't want to tell you what to write. We are simply opening the door to help you build your own ideas.

There's a lot of information here, so try to explore at your own pace, let it sink in, and then see what is triggered in your imagination.

Fiction inspires real life change. When the public can envision a future world, there is a push to make it a reality.

EARLY 20TH CENTURY
SCI-FI WRITERS WRITE
AN EXPLOSION OF STORIES
ABOUT SPACE TRAVEL

THERE IS A COLLECTIVE
PUBLIC DRIVE TO MAKE
THESE VISIONS REAL

GOVERNMENTS INVEST IN
SPACE PROGRAMS

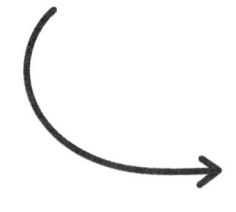

WE REACH THE MOON
VERY EARLY IN OUR
TECHNOLOGICAL
ADVANCEMENT AS A
SPECIES

THE PATH FROM FICTION TO REALITY

WOMEN CAMPAIGNING TO GET THE VOTE IN BRITAIN FOUND THE 'WOMEN WRITERS SUFFRAGE LEAGUE' IN 1908 TO ENCOURAGE WRITERS TO INCLUDE THE SUFFRAGE MOVEMENT IN PUBLICATIONS

POETRY, ARTICLES, ESSAYS, SHORT STORIES, NOVELS & PLAYS ARE PUBLISHED BY WOMEN IN UNPRECEDENTED NUMBERS

THE OUTFLOW OF PRO-SUFFRAGE WORK KEEPS DISCOURSE IN THE NEWSPAPERS, AT THE FOREFRONT OF ATTENTION

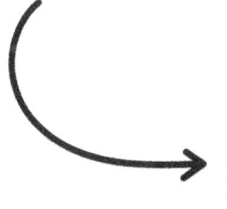

AFTER WWI, IN 1918, WOMEN IN BRITAIN RECEIVE THE VOTE

Now we have the privilege of being involved in creating the future we want to see become reality!

THE NEXT WAVE OF CLIMATE STORIES

CURRENT CLIMATE STORIES

> ### SOUND THE ALARM
> What is the climate crisis and
> how does it make us feel?

THE NEXT WAVE OF CLIMATE STORIES

> ### JUSTICE
> Why are we here and who is really
> accountable?

> ### JOURNEY
> How are we navigating out of here?

> ### WORLD-BUILDING
> Where are we heading?

The climate crisis is an epic story of the transformations that will take place across society over the coming decades. We can illuminate the routes out of the burning forest, right wrongs, and have fun exploring what a life-sustaining world might look like.

This page is based on Climate Spring's Storytelling guide
climate-spring.org

Comic by Dinos and Comics
(James Stewart and K Roméy)
and Rewriting Earth
rewriting.earth

ABOUT ME

FAVOURITE BOOKS:

FAVOURITE GENRES:

FAVOURITE WORDS:

ABOUT ME

WAYS I'VE BEEN AFFECTED BY CLIMATE CHANGE:

THINGS WHICH MAKE ME FEEL HOPEFUL:

RECENT CONVERSATIONS ABOUT CLIMATE CHANGE

NAME	THEIR PERSPECTIVE ON CLIMATE CHANGE

CLIMATE DREAMS &
FUTURE HOPES

Gaining more information about the enormity of the fight ahead of us can lead to greater feelings of anxiety and grief. Use these pages to log your changing emotions as you develop your project.

If you need support, please reach out to organisations such as:

- Climate Psychology Alliance (climatepsychologyalliance.org)
- Climate Mental Health (climatementalhealth.net)
- The Resilience Project (theresilienceproject.org.uk/resources)
- Climate Awakening (climateawakening.org)
- Good Grief Network (goodgriefnetwork.org/10steps)
- Crisis Text Line (crisistextline.org/topics/climate-anxiety-resources)

Directing your anxiety towards proactive goals can be soothing, but when a task feels as impossible as this, it often isn't enough. Please protect your mental health while doing the important work of helping our planet.

CLIMATE ANXIETIES
& GRIEF

CORE BELIEFS

MY WRITING ROUTINE

MY INSPIRATIONS & ROLE MODELS

WHEN FUTURE
GENERATIONS LOOK
BACK UPON THE GREAT
DERANGEMENT THEY
WILL CERTAINLY BLAME
THE LEADERS AND
POLITICIANS FOR THEIR
FAILURE TO ADDRESS
THE CLIMATE CRISIS. BUT
THEY MAY WELL HOLD
ARTISTS AND WRITERS
TO BE EQUALLY
CULPABLE - FOR THE
IMAGINING OF
POSSIBILITIES IS NOT
AFTER ALL, THE JOB OF
POLITICIANS AND
BUREAUCRATS.

AMITAV GHOSH

MY WRITING PROJECT

TITLE:

DATE BEGUN:

WRITING TARGETS:

PROGRESS TRACKER

FIRST DRAFT

0%	100%

STRUCTURAL EDITS & REVISIONS

0%	100%

LINE EDITS

0%	100%

0%	100%

0%	100%

0%	100%

0%	100%

ELEVATOR PITCH

COMPARISON TITLES

PROJECT MANIFESTO

What is your goal with your project? Do you want to inspire action in a call-to-arms? Is it a commercial project? Is it educational, entertaining, or both? What audience are you writing for?

ARTISTIC VISION

COVER MOODBOARD

TITLE IDEAS

WISH LIST

FUTURE VISION

Where does your project's future world fit on the chart?

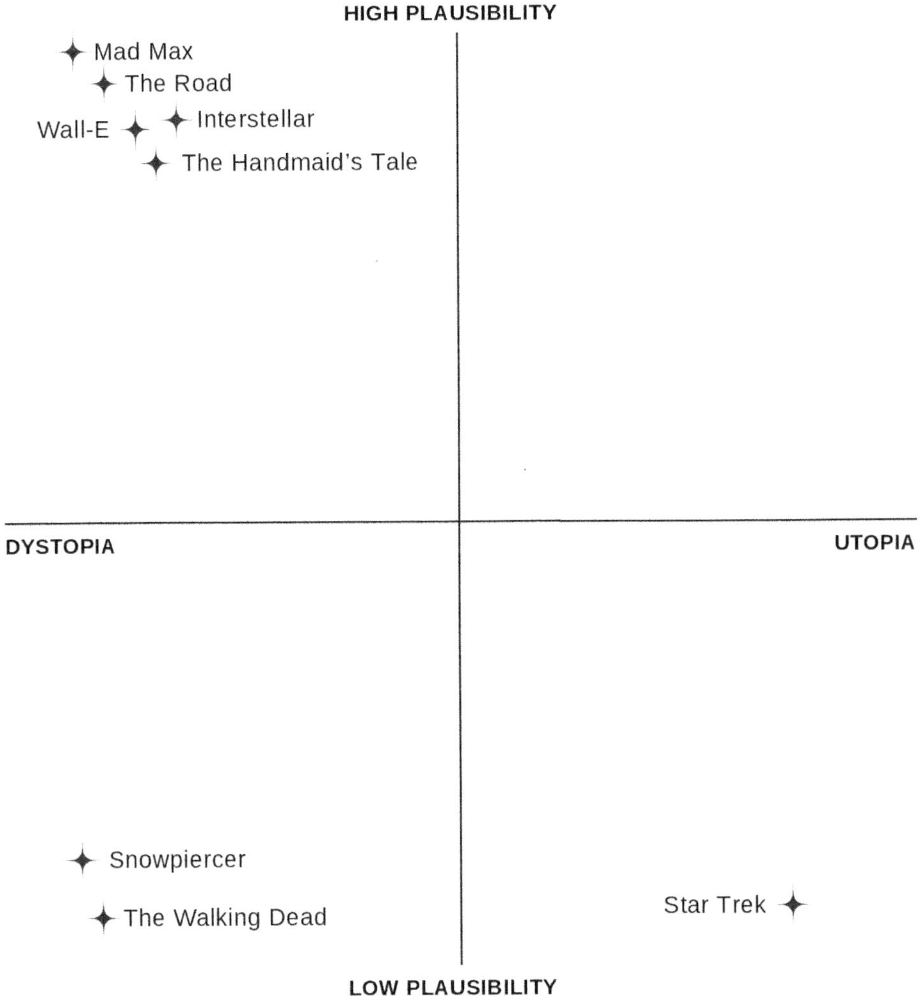

HIGH PLAUSIBILITY

✦ Mad Max
✦ The Road
Wall-E ✦ ✦ Interstellar
✦ The Handmaid's Tale

DYSTOPIA

UTOPIA

✦ Snowpiercer

✦ The Walking Dead

Star Trek ✦

LOW PLAUSIBILITY

Chart created by Steve Willis

FUTURE VISION

Where does your project's future world fit on the chart?

CLIMATE REPAIR IS PRIORITISED

CLIMATE REPAIR
AT THE COST OF
PEOPLE'S RIGHTS

ECO-HARMONY

**SOCIETAL
CONDITIONS
WORSEN**

**SOCIETAL
CONDITIONS
IMPROVE**

TOTAL
APOCALYPSE

SOCIETY
IS FAVOURED
OVER NATURE

CLIMATE REPAIR IS IGNORED

Chart developed with Pernod Ricard
pernod-ricard.com/en/media/future-scenarios-2050

WRITING INSPIRATIONS

BOOKS

MOVIES/TV

MUSIC

OTHER

WRITING INSPIRATIONS

PICTURES & MAGAZINE CUTTINGS

WRITING INSPIRATIONS

PICTURES & MAGAZINE CUTTINGS

WRITING INSPIRATIONS

QUOTATIONS

WRITING INSPIRATIONS

POETRY

WRITING INSPIRATIONS

CLIMATE NEWS REPORTS

MUSIC PLAYLIST

TITLE	ARTIST	ALBUM
e.g. The Fine Print	The Stupendium	

THE GREATEST THREAT
TO OUR PLANET IS THE
BELIEF THAT SOMEONE
ELSE WILL SAVE IT.

ROBERT SWAN

HOW TO IMPROVE YOUR CLIMATE STORYTELLING

The most effective stories are set in the present day, and demonstrate personal and collective agency at climate solutions. It's helpful if the climate solution examples are specific, do-able and combined with linked resources.

An example:

AN OKAY IDEA

A dystopian story about people dying in heat waves in the future

This doesn't help us prevent heat waves in the present day or save lives.

A BETTER IDEA

A survival story about the health impacts of heat set in the present day

This gives examples of how to treat heat impacts. However, it doesn't demonstrate systematic change.

This is adapted from 'Storytelling to Accelerate Climate Solutions' by Emily Coren

HOW TO IMPROVE YOUR CLIMATE STORYTELLING

AN EVEN BETTER IDEA

A story about individual agency, which shows a character seeking shelter in a city cooling center; learning how to install a heat pump and then assisting vulnerable neighbors.

This is a great example of individual action which shows specific and do-able behaviors.

THE BEST IDEA

A story about collective action, with many different characters working together in a variety of settings and roles. As well as installing heat pumps, they reduce urban heat islands by increasing green spaces and switching to city-wide renewable energy sources.

This is a great visualization of collective actions being taken to mitigate and adapt to heat impact.

This is adapted from 'Storytelling to Accelerate Climate Solutions' by Emily Coren

HOW TO IMPROVE YOUR CLIMATE STORYTELLING

BONUS

Add transmedia support such as social media linked to the characters in your story where audiences can <u>participate</u> in the actions that are modeled.

For example, suppose your characters get vaccinated in your story. In that case, provide a website that directs people to where they can get vaccinated in their own neighborhood.

For many examples of climate disaster resources, visit <u>unthinkable.earth/disaster-resources</u>

Remember that repetition is helpful in social learning.

The more stories that reinforce similar behaviours over more contemporary settings, the larger impacts the stories have.

Work together and often.

This is adapted from 'Storytelling to Accelerate Climate Solutions' by Emily Coren

HOW TO IMPROVE YOUR CLIMATE STORYTELLING

AN OKAY IDEA

A BETTER IDEA

THE BEST IDEA

THE CLIMATE
EMERGENCY IS THE
DEFINING HUMAN RIGHTS
ISSUE FOR THIS
GENERATION OF
CHILDREN. ITS
CONSEQUENCES WILL
SHAPE THEIR LIVES IN
ALMOST EVERY WAY
IMAGINABLE. THE
FAILURE OF MOST
✦ GOVERNMENTS TO ACT ✦
IN THE FACE OF
OVERWHELMING
SCIENTIFIC EVIDENCE IS
ARGUABLY
THE BIGGEST
INTERGENERATIONAL
HUMAN RIGHTS
VIOLATION IN HISTORY.

**AMNESTY INTERNATIONAL'S
SECRETARY GENERAL,
KUMI NAIDOO**

WEAVING CLIMATE SOLUTIONS INTO FICTION

Positive, solution-focused stories are more effective at inspiring readers than stories which focus on the problem. This leads to **avoidance, denial, fear or blaming of innocent parties.**
We shut down when faced with a potential ban or limitation. We open up when we're shown what we can gain from climate action. Focus on <u>changing social norms</u> and giving readers a <u>sense of agency,</u> rather than attempting to change attitudes and beliefs.

- Present positive visions of what a sustainable society might look like. Make it exciting, aspirational and serene. Think upgrades, not bans.

- Show high consumption lifestyles (sports cars, jet-setting) as selfish, greedy behaviours rather than something glamorous

- Try to promote green alternatives that readers might not have thought about before – especially sustainable behaviours that can be easily imitated

- Provide people with steps they can take that will uplift them and get them excited about sustainability

These pages are based on the Green Stories Project by Denise Baden
greenstories.org.uk

Sharing or borrowing instead of buying

If your protagonist is short of money, they could rent out their car on an app and make a fortune... until someone uses their car to commit a crime!

> They could visit a local 'Library of Things' to rent tools, toys or games – and get drawn into a dramatic event while trying to track down a missing community item

IDEAS FOR STORYLINES

Repair and Re-use

Anytime a character might need to buy something, can you show them repairing what they already have instead of buying new?

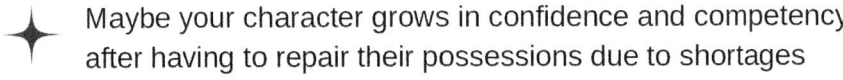 Maybe your character grows in confidence and competency after having to repair their possessions due to shortages

'Microplastics' are a common buzzword in the news, but many people aren't aware that they are created when we wash polyester clothes, releasing microplastics into the water supply. This is why it's so important to avoid cheap, plastic-based 'fast fashion'.

How about a rom-com about an intern at a fashion company which uses non-plastic fabrics? The Devil Wears Bamboo! There is even a project called FabriCandy that turns plant-based cellulose fabric scraps into glucose sugar sweets.

Show the benefits: we can reduce our exposure to toxins, especially in children, as well as saving money

These pages are based on the Green Stories Project by Denise Baden
greenstories.org.uk

The Law

Who doesn't love a legal drama? What about one set at a legal firm like ClientEarth, which uses the law to hold polluting companies and negligent governments accountable for the climate and nature crises.

Think outside the box. What if we gave the oceans a legal, national status that gives them constitutional rights which must be protected? What would it be like to be the representative for the entire Atlantic Ocean?

IDEAS FOR STORYLINES

Universal Public Transport

If your novel is set in the future, perhaps there are no private cars but electrified, quiet, on-demand buses (Uber style!), or rentable neighbourhood cars.

 How much more independence would this give teen characters who are currently reliant on lifts?

 Show the benefits: zero fossil fuels, no exhaust, fast, quiet, and cool new technology!

IDEAS FOR STORYLINES

These pages are based on the Green Stories Project by Denise Baden
greenstories.org.uk

Biodiversity

Help readers to understand that microorganisms in the soil are essential to the ecosystem. We need healthy food and farming systems which prioritise health for people and planet.

- Show farmers using pesticide- and fertiliser-free methods of growing crops, such as tree-intercropping and free-roaming livestock.

- Promote local food for local people, grown in concert with local ecosystems. Show urban farms, community gardens and farmers markets.

- Show greywater systems and water butts being used to catch rainwater.

IDEAS FOR STORYLINES

These pages are based on the Green Stories Project by Denise Baden
greenstories.org.uk

The Circular Economy

Show characters finding ways to mimic natural processes and limit their waste.

 You could include characters using a counter-top composting pot for vegetable peels while cooking in the kitchen. Later they could overhear a plot-relevant conversation while adding the waste to a garden compost bin, or gossip with neighbours while using the fresh soil to enrich their growing vegetable seedlings.

 Even hair cuttings can be added to potted plants so they grow faster – something that could be useful for DNA testing at a crime scene!

IDEAS FOR STORYLINES

These pages are based on the Green Stories Project by Denise Baden
greenstories.org.uk

Sustainable Food

Show how quick, cheap and easy it is to cook healthy, low carbon food from scratch.

- What about a baking show where one of the ingredients is cricket flour? (Yes, one sustainable solution is getting our protein from insects rather than meat!)

- What would it like to be a chef in a highly competitive "Green-Starred" Michelin restaurant, where they must reduce food waste to keep their star rating? Food waste is 10% of emissions, after all!

- Show characters saving and eating leftovers, or using apps like 'Too Good to Go' to collect leftover food from restaurants.

IDEAS FOR STORYLINES

These pages are based on the Green Stories Project by Denise Baden
greenstories.org.uk

Green Energy

What if every house, car and electrical device was powered by solar panels? An action movie-style car chase would look completely different in an eco-city. Imagine James Bond persuing a villain over rooftops covered in solar panels or vegetable farms!

 Consider the cinematic potential of a scene set amongst wind turbines or on a floating tidal generator

 Characters will have the freedom to be self-sufficient if they have an independent power supply - does this mean it's easier or harder for them to disappear 'off the grid'?

IDEAS FOR STORYLINES

WEAVING CLIMATE SOLUTIONS INTO FICTION

A Care-based Economy

Currently, the success of society is based on rates of production and consumption. How would our social values change if governments were judged on a Wellbeing or Happy Planet index instead? Imagine a world where we prioritise the wellbeing of people and planet ahead of growth. Where we invest in homecare workers, childcare providers, and family caregivers - the people who build community and strengthen connections.

Rather than a world where the strongest survive, we need one where we're all in it together.

Transformative governance systems can harness the creativity of humanity to build a completely new kind of politics, where we give power to those with wisdom, and wisdom to those with power.

As well as small community activities, imagine the workings of the larger parts of society and the economy.

How does politics work? Where does the money in the economy come from and go to? Which industries no longer exist? What is new? Build a world that you could imagine living in.

These pages are based on the Green Stories Project by Denise Baden
greenstories.org.uk

IN THE PAST I USED TO
PICK UP BEAUTIFUL STONES
ON THE BEACH

I FELT SO SATISFIED

@ JUST COMICS / JOAN CHAN

NOW I PICK UP
DIFFERENT THINGS

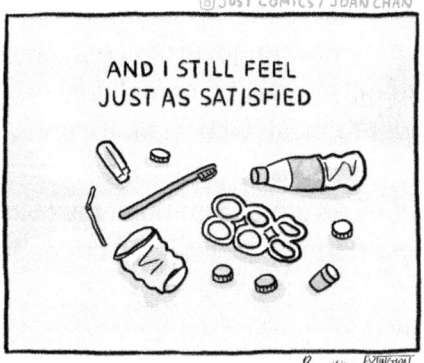

AND I STILL FEEL
JUST AS SATISFIED

Rewriting EXTINCTION

Comic by Joan Chan (Just comics)
rewriting.earth

CLIMATE SOLUTIONS CHECKLIST

Which area of climate solutions are you most interested in exploring? The most essential Stage 1 actions, where we protect Earth's biosphere, or the Stage 2 and Stage 3 actions, which focus on society and the economy?

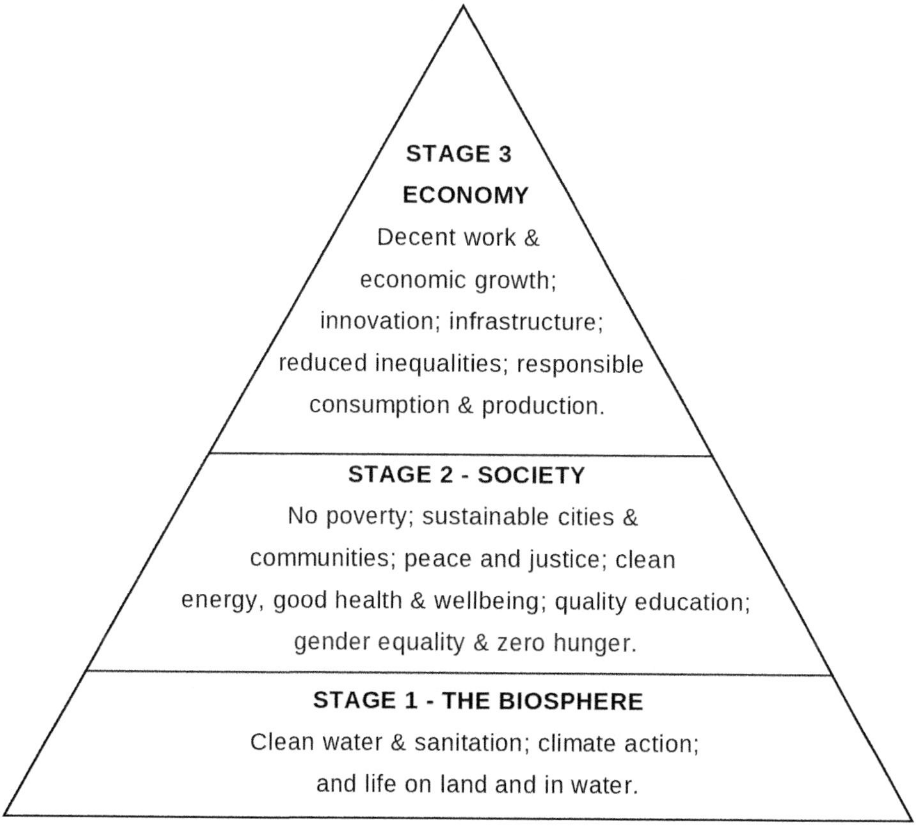

STAGE 3
ECONOMY
Decent work & economic growth; innovation; infrastructure; reduced inequalities; responsible consumption & production.

STAGE 2 - SOCIETY
No poverty; sustainable cities & communities; peace and justice; clean energy, good health & wellbeing; quality education; gender equality & zero hunger.

STAGE 1 - THE BIOSPHERE
Clean water & sanitation; climate action; and life on land and in water.

This page is based on the Sustainable Development Goals wedding cake by the Stockholm Resilience Centre
stockholmresilience.org

How many Climate Solutions have you included in your writing project?

THE BIOSPHERE

- ○ Tropical Forest Restoration
- ○ Silvopasture
- ○ Peatland Protection & Rewetting
- ○ Forest Restoration
- ○ Perennial Staple Crops
- ○ Regenerative Annual Cropping
- ○ Tree Intercropping
- ○ Managed Grazing
- ○ Multistrata Agroforestry
- ○ Conservation Agriculture
- ○ Recycling
- ○ Improved Rice Production
- ○ Indigenous Peoples' Forest Tenure
- ○ Bamboo Production
- ○ Roadside fruit & nut orchards
- ○ Free-roaming Livestock on Farmland
- ○ Seafloor Protection
- ○ Refrigerant Alternatives
- ○ Efficient Ocean Shipping
- ○ Methane Digesters
- ○ Landfill Methane Capture
- ○ Ocean sea floor and dead zone restoration
- ○ Forest Fire Management
- ○ Permafrost protection

CLIMATE SOLUTIONS CHECKLIST

SOCIETY

- ○ Reduced Food Waste
- ○ Plant-Rich Diets
- ○ Family Planning and Education
- ○ Onshore Wind Turbines
- ○ Solar Photovoltaics
- ○ Clean Cooking Stoves
- ○ Methane Leak Management
- ○ Concentrated Solar Power
- ○ LED Lighting
- ○ Offshore Wind Turbines
- ○ Efficient Trucks
- ○ Electric Cars
- ○ Waste to Energy
- ○ Geothermal Power
- ○ Aquaponics food systems
- ○ Waste to Energy
- ○ Rewilding urban areas
- ○ Land & Ocean Stewardship Governments

ECONOMY

- ○ Green city planning
- ○ Female Education
- ○ Environmental Reparations
- ○ Universal basic income
- ○ Vertical skyscraper farms
- ○ Free public transport
- ○ Free building insulation upgrades
- ○ Building Automation Systems
- ○ Green New Deal
- ○ Carpooling
- ○ High-Performance Glass
- ○ Alternative Cement
- ○ Smart Thermostats
- ○ High-Efficiency Heat Pumps
- ○ Jobs Guarantee
- ○ Modern Monetary Theory (MMT)
- ○ Local Currencies
- ○ Debt Jubilee
- ○ Participatory planning
- ○ Donut Economics
- ○ Climate Bonds
- ○ Carbon Quantitative Easing
- ○ Utilising pension funds for long-term action

Find out more about the most impactful climate solutions at drawdown.org

LISTS TEND TO BE FAR
MORE BORING THAN
STORIES. WE FIND IT
DIFFICULT TO REMEMBER
LISTS. EVOLUTION HAS
ADAPTED OUR BRAINS
TO BE GOOD AT
ABSORBING, RETAINING,
AND PROCESSING EVEN
VERY LARGE QUANTITIES
OF INFORMATION WHEN
THEY ARE SHAPED INTO
A STORY.

YUVAL NOAH HARARI

There are other climate solution ideas which are more experimental. We have no way of testing these concepts, so we don't know if they would help or hinder the planet. Which makes them interesting fodder for stories!

These 'geoengineering' techniques focus on lowering atmospheric heating and carbon levels without changing our current emissions.

Geoengineering to Reflect Sunlight Back into Space

- Launch reflective space mirrors into orbit

- Spray reflective salt water aerosols into clouds

- Inject reflective tiny air bubbles into the ocean

- Genetically modify crops to reflect light

- Cover large deserts, tundras, mountaintops and roofs in reflective materials

- Thin out wispy, high-altitude clouds to allow heat to escape into space

- Spray sulfur dioxide and other aerosols into the stratosphere to block the sunlight

Geoengineering to Capture Carbon Dioxide

- Genetically modify plants to store more carbon dioxide

- Suck carbon dioxide out of the air and inject it underground (carbon offsetting)

- Increase phytoplankton growth by . . .
    - . . . pumping nutrient-rich deep ocean water up to the sea surface
    - . . . scattering powdered iron on the ocean surface

- Spread crushed rocks onto farmland, beaches and oceans, to react with atmospheric carbon dioxide

- Restore biodiversity in 'deadzone' areas of nature.

Consider carefully how you use these concepts! Geoengineering has no track record. All these ideas would come with huge risks and unknown effects. They could...

- provide a quick fix that validates our fossil fuel use
- use huge amounts of energy and money
- benefit some countries immensely whilst harming other regions
- exploit huge areas of land and ocean
- wipe out ecosystems

But many people think that we have no choice. We might need large-scale solutions to undo the damage we've done at an industrial scale.

At the very least, discussing these shocking geoengineering concepts can help wake people up to the severity of the climate crisis.

"ONE OF THE MOST FUNDAMENTAL PRINCIPLES OF SCIENTIFIC INVESTIGATION IS THAT AN EXPERIMENT HAS TO BE ABLE TO BE REPLICATED TO GET THE SAME RESULTS, OR BASED ON THE DATA, TO CHANGE THE EXPERIMENT. GEOENGINEERING DOESN'T ALLOW FOR THAT. YOU GET ONE SHOT, AND THEN YOU LIVE WITH THE RESULTS. THAT'S NOT SCIENCE. THAT'S GAMBLING."

EXTRAPOLATIONS (APPLE TV, 2023)

THE 'UNTESTED' CLIMATE SOLUTIONS

STORYLINES ABOUT GEOENGINEERING BEING SUCCESSFUL

STORYLINES ABOUT GEOENGINEERING BEING UNSUCCESSFUL

HOW MY CHARACTERS FEEL ABOUT GEOENGINEERING

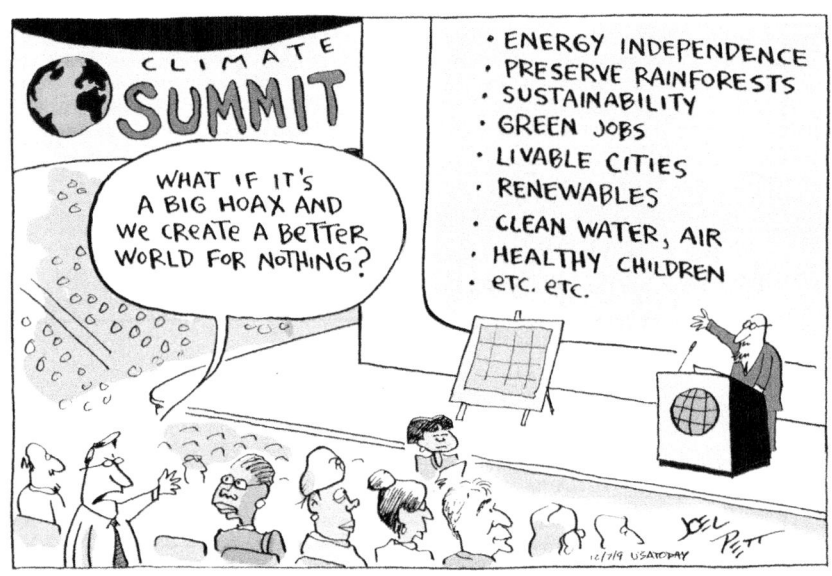

Comic by Joel Pett

THE NEED FOR COLLABORATION

If you're feeling overwhelmed by the vast amount of research you need to do for your project, consider reaching out to an expert for input and feedback. Often they will be delighted to help you. People love talking about their research and passion projects!

Some tips:

- Look for someone who has the skills you lack - if you are creative and literary, you might want to find a collaborator who is more technical-minded, to spot the gaps in your ideas from a logical perspective
- Go niche. Find experts in the most specific field you can. Look on LinkedIn for professionals working on mangrove forests or Arctic albedo management, rather than reaching out to general climate advisors.
- Tell people what you're working on, and what you'd like from them. Be clear about what you can offer in return: a chance to showcase their work in your writing!
- Expect a low response rate. Email 100 people in the hope that a meaningful discussion will arise with 1 person.
- Ask anyone who responds if they could connect you with other people who might be keen to be involved in your project.
- Make sure you acknowledge their contribution in an afterword.

THE NEED FOR
COLLABORATION

Here's a template you can use to reach out for help on your project.

Hello _____!

I'm a writer currently working on a climate fiction project. I'm developing a storyline about _____. I was wondering if you had time to discuss your work in this area. The things you're working on with _____ are really exciting, and I'd love to hear more about this. In particular, I'd like to learn more about

_____.

I'd also be interested to hear your vision of a positive future. What would you like to see happen over the next few decades? I'd love to weave your ideas into my project to help manifest them.

I'm not a technical expert, so any help you could give me in turning complicated ideas into easy-to-understand concepts would be really appreciated. I think it's really important to showcase climate solutions in fiction, to help raise awareness of the next steps we need to take as a society. I'd be happy to tell you a bit more about my project if that would be helpful.

No worries at all if you don't have the capacity for this - I know you're very busy! But I thought I'd reach out and ask. I'd love to be connected with anyone else you think might be able to help me too. Thank you for your time. I really appreciate it. Keep up the important work!

TO INSPIRE PEOPLE, WE
NEED TO TELL A STORY
NOT OF SACRIFICE AND
DEPRIVATION BUT OF
OPPORTUNITY AND
IMPROVEMENT IN OUR
LIVES, OUR HEALTH AND
OUR WELL-BEING - A
STORY OF HUMANS
FLOURISHING IN A
POST-FOSSIL-FUEL AGE.

SUSAN JOY HASSOL

CLIMATE STORY FRAMES

TODAY'S DOMINANT CLIMATE STORY

> ### EARNED DYSTOPIA
> e.g. The Day After Tomorrow, Don't Look Up,
> Wall-E, Mad Max, Snowpiercer

By understanding what audiences care about most, we can create stories that resonate across belief and political spectrums.

Doomsday stories set in apocalyptic worlds can attract attention, but rarely lead to genuine personal engagement. They make people feel hopeless, overwhelmed and distanced from the issue.

If you are writing a survival story, bear in mind that talking about distant, abstract, planetary-level consequences is less impactful than showing issues which are **local and immediate**, such as:
- shortages or price-hikes in food and water
- days where it's too hot or polluted to go outside
- high air conditioning bills
- extreme fires

These pages are based on Futerra's 'Stories to Save the World' guide
wearefuterra.com

CLIMATE
STORY FRAMES

AN EARNED DYSTOPIA STORYLINE

HOW THIS COULD BE ADJUSTED TO MAKE
PEOPLE FEEL LESS HOPELESS

CLIMATE STORY FRAMES

STORIES ABOUT RISING UP AGAINST DOOM

> ### YOUTH MUTINY
> ### AGAINST EXPLOITATION
> e.g. The Hunger Games, Green Rising

> ### TECHNO SAVIOUR
> e.g. Iron Man, Big Hero 6

> ### GLOBAL AWAKENING TO CREATE A NEW
> ### WORLD OF ECO-HARMONY
> e.g. Eat Pray Love

Everyone loves a shiny, quick-fix, jargon-laden solution - whether it's led by a plucky girl leader, tech saviour or mystic advisor.

But be careful, as these stories can breed complacency, distract attention from real solutions or help justify dangerous geoengineering projects.

These pages are based on Futerra's 'Stories to Save the World' guide and the article 'Strategic narratives in climate change: Towards a unifying narrative to address the action gap on climate change' by Simon Bushell et al.

CLIMATE
STORY FRAMES

A YOUTH MUTINY STORYLINE

A TECH SAVIOUR STORYLINE

A GLOBAL AWAKENING STORYLINE

NEW NARRATIVES TO REACH
NEW AUDIENCES

MESSY UTOPIAS
e.g. Futurama, Star Trek,
A Psalm for the Wild-Built

Most positive visions generated by environmentalists are sexless, boring, hermetically-sealed shells.

Instead, **we need emotional, intense stories set in believable, desirable, nuanced worlds filled with jeopardy and excitement.**

However, bear in mind that these stories can be met with resistance if they ask individuals to deviate from the social norm or put aside their preferences and habits. **Frame lifestyle changes as upgrades rather than restrictions.**

These pages are based on Futerra's 'Stories to Save the World' guide, and the article 'Strategic narratives in climate change: Towards a unifying narrative to address the action gap on climate change' by Simon Bushell et al

CLIMATE
STORY FRAMES

A MESSY UTOPIA STORYLINE

HOW THE WORLD WILL BE DESIRABLE

HOW THE WORLD WILL BE MESSY

INDIGENOUS & TRADITIONAL
STORY AS GUIDE
e.g. Sand Talk, the Greenlandic Mother of
the Sea, the Menominee Legend of Spirit
Rock, the Enchanted Lakes of the Amazon

Across the world, indigenous, traditional narratives hold the secret to healing the division between people and nature. How can we all uplift indigenous storytellers with our stories?

Respect the cultural dimensions of stories and try to **positively represent minorities in ways that communicate their knowledge, skills and strengths.**

Think about what your story can achieve for diverse communities. Is it about building representation and amplifying voices? Or giving insight into community perspectives to highlight the need for policy and resources?

These pages are based on Futerra's 'Stories to Save the World' guide and tips by Judy Ling Wong, the President of the Black Environment Network

CLIMATE
STORY FRAMES

Jobs which are fulfilled in majority by People of Colour (farmworkers, food supply chain workers, and domestic/direct care workers) are more likely to be exposed to:

- high emissions and poor air quality
- a lack of clean water access
- hotter temperatures and more flooding
- a lack of governmental disaster support
- workplace pesticides and pollutants
- long work hours and low wages
- a risk of deportation or job loss if they voice their concerns

In an emergency, they must choose between risking their lives or giving up the wages they need. They are often on the front lines of cleaning up after disasters in dangerous conditions.

Natural resource extraction is also directly linked to violence against (largely Indigenous) women and LGBTQ+ people, when well-paid outsiders enter remote, rural communities, with no ties to the place or its people.

These issues are complex, so make sure you research and learn from the viewpoints of real people before writing about their experiences.

This page is based on Storyline Partners'
'Writing About The Climate Crisis: Work, Workers and Care'
storylinepartners.com/resources/

CLIMATE
STORY FRAMES

A DIVERSE, INCLUSIVE STORYLINE

HOW I CAN REPRESENT
INDIGENOUS PERSPECTIVES

HOW I CAN HIGHLIGHT THE SKILLS OF
TRADITIONAL COMMUNITIES

NORMALISING SUSTAINABLE ACTIVITY
e.g. Falling Inn Love, Ted Lasso (Season 2,
Episode 3)

Living sustainably isn't yet normal (however much we think it should be). But many other things also weren't normal once – like divorce, designated drivers and women in the workplace.

Gentle sit-coms help normalise and humanise new ways of living. A gentle comedy about climate action could be beautifully subversive.

However, be careful not to focus too much on stories about small, individual actions. The idea that 'every little bit helps' can make people feel frustrated, since it feels like these changes can't possibly make any difference. This leaves audiences isolated rather than part of a bigger community working together.

These pages are based on Futerra's 'Stories to Save the World' guide and the article 'Strategic narratives in climate change: Towards a unifying narrative to address the action gap on climate change' by Simon Bushell et al

A GENTLE SIT-COM IDEA

HOW I CAN MAKE CLIMATE SOLUTIONS COMEDIC

HOW I CAN WEAVE CLIMATE SOLUTIONS INTO A LOW-STAKES PLOTLINE

THRUTOPIA
e.g. Fairhaven

We need clear, engaging routes **'through'** to a world we'd all be proud to bequeath to future generations. If we're going to write a world that functions differently, we need to get granular. Stories must dig deep into the mechanics, to map a clear path from here to there.

We need to know how things work: **how we generate power, how we use money, how we organise our politics differently, and how we feed ourselves.**

Historically, we know we are capable of working at a phenomenal pace when the mindset is there to take action (the USA made 7 warships a day during WWII!). We are now in massive communal peril. What could we achieve if we all took a warfooting?

This page is based on the Thrutopia Masterclass
thrutopia.life

CLIMATE
STORY FRAMES

A THRUTOPIA IDEA

WHAT WILL BE DIFFERENT 5 YEARS AFTER MY STORY ENDS

WHAT WILL BE DIFFERENT 10 YEARS AFTER MY STORY ENDS

CLIMATE
STORY FRAMES

ACTION AS ADVENTURE
AND COMMUNITY
e.g. The Lord of the Rings, The Wild Robot,
Dune, Ragnarok (TV show)

Reaching a sustainable, regenerative future can be a thrilling adventure. If told as a 'heroic journey', it could include unexpected allies, inciting incidents, setbacks, and compelling races against time. Stories of re-world-building can be epics with change, upheaval and inner strength.

However, be careful not to create predominantly white characters who confront and solve issues by being the "natural" leader/hero. Make your main characters caregivers, domestic workers or food supply chain workers. Consider having an ensemble cast who are made up of dedicated, passionate community members.

Note that using non-human protagonists like animals or robots can contribute to the 'distancing' of climate change by portraying it as someone else's problem, far away. It can also cause cynicism and fatigue, due to being overused.

These pages are based on Futerra's 'Stories to Save the World' guide, Storyline Partners' 'Writing About The Climate Crisis: Work, Workers and Care' and the article 'Strategic narratives in climate change: Towards a unifying narrative to address the action gap on climate change' by Simon Bushell et al

CLIMATE
STORY FRAMES

AN ACTION-ADVENTURE IDEA

HEROES' CALL TO ADVENTURE

HEROES' INNER STRUGGLES & CONFLICTS

CLIMATE STORY FRAMES

HEROES' TRAINING & MENTORING MONTAGE

HEROES' FIRST CHALLENGE

HEROES' FIRST FAILURE

CLIMATE
STORY FRAMES

HEROES' FIRST VICTORY

HEROES' ULTIMATE TEST

HEROES' REWARD FOR VICTORY

CLIMATE STORY FRAMES

CHARACTER-LED CLIMATE ACTION
e.g. Erin Brockovich, Blue Planet, I am
Greta, To the End, Before the Flood

There are millions of fascinating, funny, crazy, brave and wonderful people fighting uphill battles to save the world. From climate justice warriors to lifestyle gurus, we need more people to model.

Rather than lionising the techno-bros, how about the soccer moms taking on big coal, or the First Nations saving rivers?

Fictionalise real stories. Show collective organising, such as worker unionisation; community-based caregiving and neighborhoods supporting climate crisis refugees or disaster survivors.

These small seeds of stories can be pinpoints of light in the gloom and doom.

These pages are based on Futerra's Stories to Save the World and Storyline Partners' 'Writing About The Climate Crisis: Work, Workers and Care'

A CHARACTER-LED IDEA

REAL LIFE INSPIRATION STORIES

e.g. Juliana v. United States – a lawsuit filed in 2015 by 21 youth plaintiffs against the US government, as their affirmative actions that cause climate change have violated the youngest generation's constitutional rights to life, liberty, and property

CLIMATE POETRY

As with stories, poetry can be used to write the future into being. It can help us tackle the dark and difficult challenges of the present day with a spirit of stubborn optimism. Poetry can express intention and longing: to change our belief in ourselves to make a future for Earth.

It crosses genres and allows us to meet each other openly in our struggles, link arms, wipe our tears and choose a liveable future on Earth.

Traditonal forms of climate poetry:
- **The Nature Poem** - poetry inspired by the natural world
- **The Praise Poem** - poems as ode or tribute, expressing gratitude
- **Ecopoetry** - poetry with strong environmental messaging

The next generation of climate poetry:
- **Thrutopoetry** - poetry that leads us through to the future we want to create. A thrutopoem might explain how to fit a solar panel, but only if the solar panel is on your heart. It might world-build a community living a solarpunked life that makes you leap up and shout: I want that!

From Bending The Arc: A Thrutopia Magazine
bendingthearcmagazine.substack.com

CLIMATE POETRY

Salvage, recycle and retrofit existing poetry forms, facts and language into new structures.

Good poetry can:
- Yearn for or mourn old certainties
- Use a tone of urgency or purpose
- Foreground adaptation and innovation
- Focus on our personal and collective agency to choose a flourishing future
- Show ways humans create resilient communities
- Mend separation from the animate earth
- Focus on the path forward which is alive and full of potential

Keep in mind what you can do to bring poetry to your message and open up a way through to a better future.

Spark joy.

Accept unpredictability and turbulence as being foundational to the times we're living in, but don't dwell in that fear.

From Bending The Arc: A Thrutopia Magazine
bendingthearcmagazine.substack.com

CLIMATE
POETRY

'The Thrutopian Shovel' is an activity developed to help make a climate poem. It borrows a factual quote or phrase about the climate crisis, and uses it as the last word of each line in a poem. If you only read the last words down the length of the poem, you'll be reading the original quotation. Give it a try!

YOUR POEM

INSPIRATIONAL QUOTE

HOW TO AVOID BEING PREACHY

Create stories that offer a multitude of readings. It's important to let your readers make up their own minds about the climate and not preach to them. Readers value stories a lot more if they have creative input.

When writing about something you feel strongly about, it can be hard not to tell your readers what to do. But propaganda has a much shorter range and shelf-life than something that is elusive and curious.

A 'READERLY' TEXT

Every piece of information and intellectual and emotional reaction is provided by the story. All that the reader needs to do is show up and passively read the words and the job is done for them.

A 'WRITERLY' TEXT

A story in which the reader needs to get actively involved and work with the text to create the meaning for themselves. This is where the proper pleasure of reading happens.

This page is based on work from 'We all die at the end' by Sam Haddow
Roland Barthes innovated the concept of 'writerly' vs 'readerly' texts (1970)

Readers come to texts in their own way, with their own needs and expectations. Storytellers can never maintain control of how their stories will land.

Stories that try to force us to respond and feel in a particular way leave no space for engagement. Entrust your readers with the space to find their own way through them. The environmental messages will hit harder because of it.

A 'READERLY' STORY IDEA

A 'WRITERLY' STORY IDEA

This page is based on work from 'We all die at the end' by Sam Haddow
Roland Barthes innovated the concept of 'writerly' vs 'readerly' texts (1970)

TIPS TO AVOID BEING DIDACTIC

Stealth Exposition

Avoid info-dumping. If people feel like they are just a 'lay person' who will never know as much as the experts, it prevents them from gaining ownership of the problem.

Do your research, but avoid *showing* your research.

Find ways to sneak in the essential information in a way that doesn't disrupt the world of the story. Dramatise it.

 Use your ensemble cast of characters to relate information. Mentor figures can often be useful for imparting wisdom – the Merlins and Obi-Wan Kenobis – whether true or false.

IDEAS FOR SIDE CHARACTERS' DIALOGUE

These pages are based on work from 'Writing Ecofiction' by Kevan Manwaring (Springer, 2024)

TIPS TO AVOID BEING DIDACTIC

Use multimedia formats such as letters, emails, cryptic codes, newspaper reports, radio broadcasts or treasure maps to slip in information in ways that add texture.

IDEAS FOR MULTIMEDIA POSTS

The Democracy of Character

Create a healthy cross-section of characters who represent a spectrum of beliefs and stances.

Give space for the reader to decide who they agree and disagree with, who they relate to and who they do not.

These pages are based on work from 'Writing Ecofiction' by Kevan Manwaring (Springer, 2024)

Dramatise a healthy debate between positions – otherwise you risk biasing one particular stance, or not fairly representing the cross-section of opinions (and possibly alienating your reader).

IDEAS FOR CHARACTER DEBATES

(Don't) Bend the Plot

When it feels characters have no agency, but are merely pawns that progress the writer's goals, the reader stops believing in them, and therefore stop caring for them.

Plot should emerge out of characters' actions and develop in an organic way.

These pages are based on work from 'Writing Ecofiction' by Kevan Manwaring (Springer, 2024)

TIPS TO AVOID BEING DIDACTIC

Give characters time to make decisions at their own pace. Imagine a set of scales. One end is weighed with stifling fears, the other with enticing desires (to meet a new partner, to move to a new town, find a new job or experience something different). When the desires outweigh the fears, the character will act. If, however, the fears outweigh the desires then the character will freeze or retreat.

The most gripping writing occurs when the characters seem to come alive and stray from the 'path' allotted them. It must seem like they have a choice, and not everything is predetermined.

MOST OBVIOUS CHARACTER PATH

MOST SURPRISING CHARACTER PATH

These pages are based on work from 'Writing Ecofiction' by Kevan Manwaring (Springer, 2024)

IDEAS FOR CHARACTER DILEMMAS

Avoid Solutionism

Don't present glib solutions to the complex problems we face. There is no 'silver bullet' that can save us.

- Deploy open endings, ambivalence, messy compromises, and ongoing large-scale effort—rather than a closed, singular resolution.

IDEAS FOR OPEN ENDINGS

These pages are based on work from 'Writing Ecofiction' by Kevan Manwaring (Springer, 2024)

ACADEMIA CAN
HELP PRESERVE
KNOWLEDGE, BUT
STORIES ARE HOW
WE WEAVE
ECOLOGICAL
CONNECTIONS IN
THE FABRIC OF
COMMUNITIES.

DIANDRA MARIZET

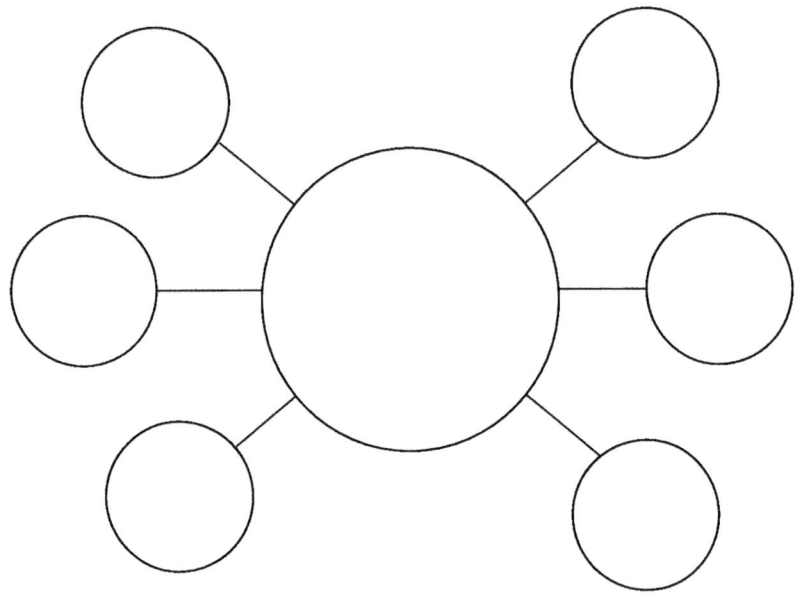

BRAINSTORMING

BRAINSTORMING

BRAINSTORMING

WRITING GOALS
CHECKLIST

- ○ Show do-able solutions
- ○ Normalise and encourage action
- ○ Focus on the big picture
- ○ Be accessible
- ○ Talk to a specific audience
- ○ Pair problems with solutions
- ○ Highlight people who are making a difference
- ○ Show characters experiencing climate grief and anxiety
- ○ Don't shy away from being provocative
- ○
- ○
- ○
- ○
- ○
- ○
- ○
- ○
- ○
- ○
- ○
- ○
- ○
- ○
- ○
- ○
- ○
- ○
- ○

Add in your own writing goals - whether it's to
finish a first draft, get published or read your
poetry at an open mic night!

I GIVE MYSELF
PERMISSION TO . . .

CREATING SPACE TO WRITE

HOW I WILL
PROGRESS MY CRAFT

HOW I WILL STRAY FROM
THE COMMON PATH

HOW I WILL TAKE RESPONSIBILITY FOR MY WRITING

Take your notebook on a walk and jot down any descriptions of natural spaces which come to mind. Glue in feathers, pressed flowers and fallen leaves!

RECENT WALKS IN NATURE

WHEN AN OLD CULTURE
IS DYING, THE NEW
CULTURE IS CREATED BY
THOSE PEOPLE WHO
ARE NOT AFRAID TO BE
INSECURE.

RUDOLF BAHRO

EFFECTS OF CLIMATE
CHANGE I'VE SEEN
IN MY AREA

HOW I WILL GIVE VOICE TO THE NATURAL WORLD

HOW I WILL BUILD RELATIONSHIPS WITH ANIMALS

WE LIVE IN
CAPITALISM. ITS
POWER SEEMS
INESCAPABLE – BUT
THEN SO DID THE
DIVINE RIGHT OF
KINGS. ANY HUMAN
POWER CAN BE
RESISTED AND
CHANGED BY HUMAN
BEINGS. RESISTANCE
AND CHANGE OFTEN
BEGIN IN ART. VERY
OFTEN IN THE ART OF
WORDS.

URSULA K LE GUIN

NOTES ON WORLD-BUILDING

THE CULTURAL NARRATIVE OF MY WORLD

Cultural narratives can shape how we see ourselves and society. For example, *Lord of the Flies* reinforces the narrative that humanity is competitive, selfish and violent, whereas *A Psalm for the Wild-Built* shows humanity as cooperative, collaborative and kind.

Consider whether your story repeats dominant narratives, or challenges and replaces them with counter narratives.

TRADITIONAL STORYTELLING & FOLKLORE

INDUSTRY AND POLITICS

NEWS HEADLINES & SOCIAL MEDIA POSTS FROM MY STORY'S WORLD

Sketch/collage/moodboard your vision for your characters' homes. Label any sustainable features, like compost bins or solar panels!

MY CHARACTER'S CITY

Sketch/collage/moodboard your vision for your characters' city or village. Label any sustainable features, like cycle lanes or vertical farms!

MY CHARACTER'S WORLD

NOTES ON PLOT

FORESHADOWING &
PLOT TWISTS

NOTES ON TONE

THEMES & MOTIFS

BUZZWORD BINGO

How many climate topics have you included in your writing project?

SOLASTALGIA	DEEP TIME	CORPORATE DEFLECTION	GREEN-WASHING	CLIMATE SOLUTIONS
MILITARY EMISSIONS	ANTHRO-POCENE	COLLECTIVE ACTION	DRAWDOWN	GEO-ENGINEERING
SLOW VIOLENCE	LOCAL FOOD MOVEMENT	**FREE SPACE**	CONSUMER BLAME & CARBON FOOTPRINTS	UPCYCLING
ANTI-LAWN MOVEMENT	POLITICAL BRIBERY	FOSSIL FUEL INDUSTRY DENIAL AD CAMPAIGNS	CEO CITIZENS ARRESTS	CIVIL DISOBE-DIENCE
ECOANXIETY	GRASSROOTS ORGANISERS	CLIMATE MIGRATION	THIRD WORLD ACTIVISTS	INTER-SECTION-ALITY

Climate buzzwords can come with a lot of emotional baggage. Using complex terms or acronyms also means your readers might have to pause to look things up, taking them out of their immersion in your work.

How can you consider the wording you use in your project to make it more uplifting or easier to understand? Brainstorm terms you could change or make more descriptive. For example, instead of 'ban' you could say 'upgrade'. Instead of 'sustainable' you could say 'safe and healthy'. Try not to use 'climate' as an adjective (e.g. climate jobs, climate action).

Renewables	**Clean power**
Emissions	
Carbon Neutral	
Net Zero	
Biodiversity	
Carbon Tax	
Deforestation	
Lifestyle changes	
Green New Deal	
Offsetting	
Sacrifice	

This page is based on 'Talk Like a Human' by Potential Energy

NOTES ON CHARACTER

CHARACTER JOB IDEAS

- Plant-rich chef, food truck owner or school cafeteria cook
- Community organizer
- Justice advocate
- Food bank or supermarket employee
- Sustainable farmer
- Food product entrepreneur
- Solar/wind contractor
- Architect or urban planner of green cities & buildings
- CEO switching to clean energy/ethical factories
- Civil servant working on green campaigns
- Public transit worker
- City transportation planner
- Vehicle designer
- Travel agent or tour guide
- Plastic alternatives inventor
- Waste scientist, engineer, planner
- Marine biologist or fisher
- Upcycled fashion designer or artist
- Startup making products from trash
- Community or school advocate
- Thought leader or change maker
- Investor or financial advisor
- Park ranger
- Journalist

This page is based on 'Sustainability on Screen: Character Choices, World Building & Settings'
climateonscreen.org

CHARACTER JOB IDEAS

The landscape of work is going to change immensely as the planet does. What kind of jobs will this create? Help your readers see the kinds of ordinary jobs they could be doing in the future, to show that there is a place for their skills. Deal them in, not out.

Brainstorm the kinds of workers who will be needed in 50 years in these key areas:

CLIMATE CRISIS LAND MANAGEMENT

RESOURCE & LABOUR SHORTAGE

MANAGING SHIFTING POPULATIONS & DEMOGRAPHICS (MIGRANTS, REFUGEES AND OLDER WORKFORCES)

CHARACTER JOB IDEAS

CITIZEN, CIVIL & EQUALITY ACTION

TECHNOLOGY - DATA, AI & DIGITAL

ENERGY

HEALTH

PROTAGONIST BIOGRAPHY

CHARACTER MOTIVATIONS

BACKSTORY

25 DETAILS ABOUT
MY PROTAGONIST

1
2
3
4
5
6
7
8
9
10
11
12
13
14
15
16
17
18
19
20
21
22
23
24
25

IF THIS CHARACTER HAD $50 BILLION, THEY'D USE IT TO.....

LOVE INTEREST BIOGRAPHY

ENSEMBLE CAST BIOGRAPHIES

ENSEMBLE CAST
BIOGRAPHIES

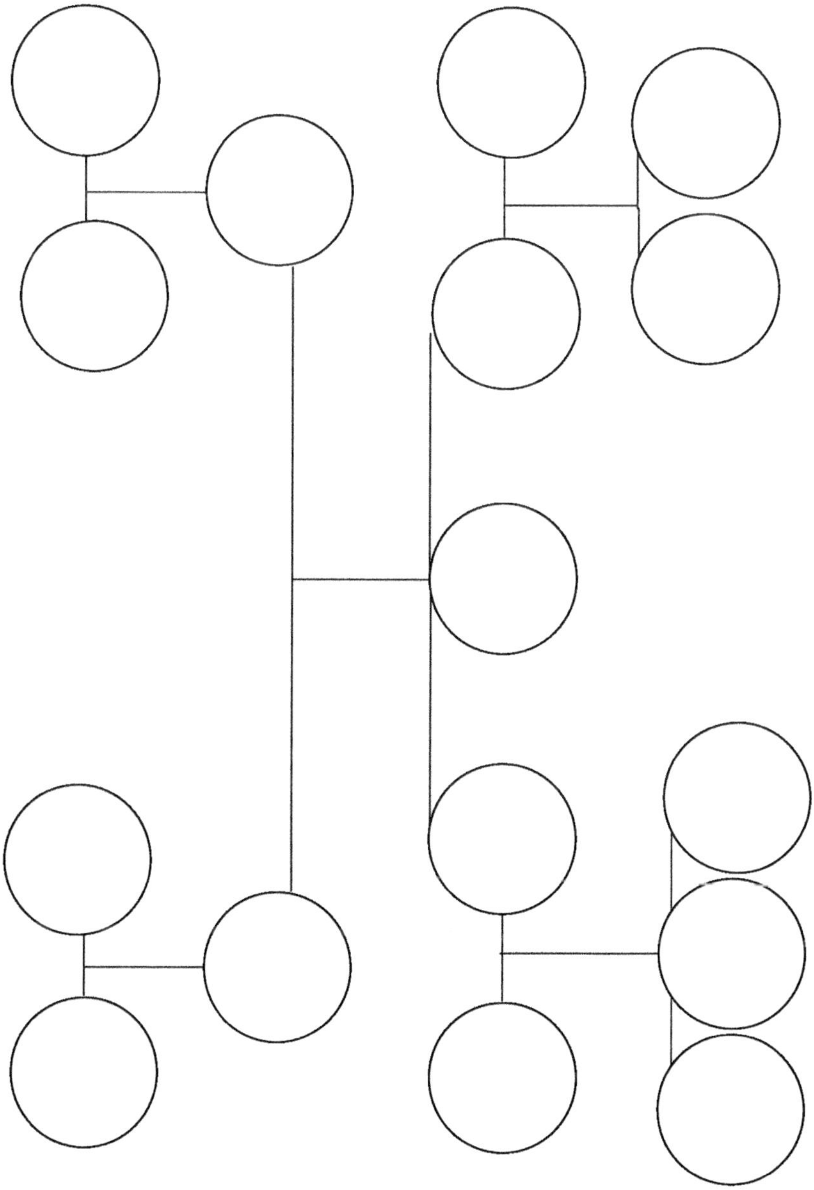

Turn sideways!

INDIVIDUAL CLIMATE ACTION CHECKLIST

How many of these could your characters do?

- ◯ Pledge to not mow lawns
- ◯ Buy secondhand clothing from charity shops/pre-loved clothes apps, go to a fashion swap, or repair existing clothes
- ◯ Air-dry clothing instead of tumble drying
- ◯ Register to vote
- ◯ Run for a local election
- ◯ Switch to LED lightbulbs
- ◯ Go foraging
- ◯ Plant a tree
- ◯ Make a bird bath, wildlife pond, bird box or insect hotel
- ◯ Volunteer for a local activism network
- ◯ Distribute activism outreach materials
- ◯ Donate to environmental or educational charities
- ◯ Switch to plant-based foods
- ◯ Change to a renewable energy utility supplier
- ◯ Sign government petitions
- ◯ Attend a protest rally
- ◯ Change to a bank which has divested from fossil fuel investments
- ◯ Speak to employers/educators about divesting pension schemes
- ◯ Initiate discussions about sustainability within work/school
- ◯ Speak to relatives/neighbours/contacts/network about how their work will become a climate solution
- ◯ Create a network of activists that fills a gap in the community (like the Climate Fiction Writers League!). Arrange events and start conversations!

Think really big – what is the biggest thing you can do? Do it, then identify the next, even bigger thing you could tackle, using the skills you have learned from previous endeavours.

By whatever means, we must fully cover any personal carbon footprints, then our family's; our forebears'; our street's; our town's; our county's; country's. Set up a company or startup that solves some of the big problems. Step forward and do uncomfortable things.

○
○
○
○
○
○
○
○
○
○
○
○
○
○
○
○
○

Add in your own ideas here!

ACTION PLAN

What is a small step, within the next 1-2 years, that can be taken to start to realize your goal?

What is a great leap, within 4-5 years, that will build momentum and turn potential into meaningful systemic change?

What is a victory condition, in 8-9 years, that will show us that meaningful change has occurred, and is continuing to unfold?

This activity was developed by the
Center for Science & the Imagination
csi.asu.edu

THE BUTTERFLY EFFECT

The common factors blamed for climate change are overconsumption, excessive population growth & mismanaged social systems. How can you incorporate these issues into new, interesting, unique characters?

Hold profit-hungry corporations and governments accountable for their actions. Focus on how unfair it is that we allow mega-corporations and militaries to pollute in a way that costs us all. Show how much better our money and health will become once we aren't dependent on dirty, expensive energy. We aren't fighting climate change. We are fighting the polluters who are causing climate change.

This page is based on 'Talk Like a Human' by Potential Energy potentialenergycoalition.org

25 DETAILS ABOUT MY ANTAGONIST

1
2
3
4
5
6
7
8
9
10
11
12
13
14
15
16
17
18
19
20
21
22
23
24
25

IF THIS CHARACTER HAD $50 BILLION, THEY'D USE IT TO.....

What is my antagonist's position in society? What power do they hold that could help or hinder climate action?

How does my antagonist justify their climate denial and/or pollution to themselves? What arguments might they bring up against climate change?

In what ways does my antagonist's power benefit society?

What emotional connections or forms of empathy could change my antagonist's perspective?

What kind of person might be able to engage in a gentle discussion of climate change with this character?

WRITING DIVERSELY

When writing about marginalised people, avoid writing stories <u>about the experience</u> of being in a minority group if you have not experienced it yourself. Include characters in your world, but don't centralise their identity. Diversity should be incidental to the story, not used as a punchline or key plot point.

Do your research!

Ask people within the minority about their experiences. Learn from others and set aside your assumptions. Try to realistically represent the real world. Consider seeking out a sensitivity reader from within the community, and listen carefully to their feedback on your work.

- Be aware of common stereotypes for the community (think about: occupations, family dynamics, backgrounds or story roles).
- Research the microagressions that people face (e.g. treating People of Colour as if they must be poor, uneducated or service staff)

Check your terminology:

- Have you included a reclaimed slur that can only be said within the community?
- Are you describing characters in ways that could appear fetishizing? (e.g. describing complexions as 'caramel' or 'chocolate', eyes as being 'slanted', hair as being 'wild' or 'untamed'). Are you <u>only</u> describing the appearance of minority characters, implying there is a straight/white/able-bodied default?

These pages are based on the 'Writing Diverse Fiction' workshop by Wren James
wrenjames.co.uk/school-visits/

Make them realistic

Give your minority characters an active role in the plot. Don't just use them to progress the narrative of the protagonist. Avoid isolated, token characters. Include a variety of characters, showcasing a range of life experiences and attitudes.

- Explicitly define identities on the page rather than just implying traits through their behaviour (e.g. Sherlock Holmes, Luna Lovegood and Spock are coded as being autistic; Disney's Ursula, Jafar and Hades are queer-coded. These are based on inaccurate stereotypes)
- By letting your characters proudly discuss and put a name on their identities, you are showing that they feel safe and accepted for who they are, and don't feel a need to censor themselves or hide away.
- Non-human characters like aliens or robots are often used as a metaphor for a diverse identity (e.g. transgender, asexual). This is an easy way to include a different type of character without having to do research. Make sure you also include real representation rather than just a fantastical substitute!

Don't romanticise them

Don't glorify people's experiences or suffering. Equally, don't 'fix' or 'rescue' them. For example, disabled characters are often miraculously cured or used as villains in stories (e.g. Darth Vader and the Joker).

WRITING DIVERSELY

Think about your reader

Everyone deserves to see themselves getting happily-ever-afters in stories, where they are the hero and are loved and accepted.

- Don't kill off minority characters! Diverse characters are commonly the first to die in fiction.
- If you include hate speech in your story, make sure it falls flat. Show the bigots as foolish and ridiculous, committing an unacceptable faux pas. Bigotry shouldn't be a central obstacle in your character's journey. Defang their attempt at control.
- Move beyond the 'coming out' or 'self-acceptance' narrative - life continues beyond someone's relationship with their identity
- Make sure you aren't exclusively using minority characters as villains

Make diversity a key part of your worldbuilding

Think about the social prejudices you choose to include in your fantasy or historical world. In a world of dragons, there doesn't need to be homophobia, or a servant class comprised of People of Colour

- Minority people have existed at all points of history, even if they were erased from the narrative. Give them back their voice

Learning how to accurately portray the diverse world around us is an essential part of the literary craft. It can improve your characterisation and storytelling in a multitude of ways.

WRITING DIVERSELY

Choose an identity you don't know much about and research real people's lives in depth. Find books from writers within the community, watch Youtube videos or look up tags on Instagram.

COMMON STEREOTYPES

3 FACTS I DIDN'T KNOW

3 FAMOUS CELEBRITIES INFLUENCERS WRITERS

These pages are based on the 'Writing Diverse Fiction' workshop by Wren James
wrenjames.co.uk/school-visits/

RECOMMENDED READING

The Climate Book by Greta Thunberg

Drawdown: The Most Comprehensive Plan Ever Proposed to Reverse Global Warming by Paul Hawken

After Geoengineering: Climate Tragedy, Repair, and Restoration by Holly Jean Buck

All We Can Save: Truth, Courage, and Solutions for the Climate Crisis by Ayana Elizabeth Johnson

How to Talk About Climate Change in a Way That Makes a Difference by Rebecca Huntley

Hope in Hell: A decade to confront the climate emergency by Jonathon Porritt

How Are We Going to Explain This?: Our Future on a Hot Earth by Jelmer Mommers

Given Half a Chance: Ten Ways to Save the World by Edward Davey

The Future We Choose: Surviving the Climate Crisis by Christiana Figueres and Tom Rivett-Carnac

There Is No Planet B: A Handbook for the Make or Break Years by Mike Berners-Lee

The Planet Remade: How Geoengineering Could Change the World by Oliver Morton

Wilding by Isabella Tree

What We Need to Do Now: For a Zero Carbon Future by Chris Goodall

This Changes Everything: Capitalism vs. The Climate by Naomi Klein

Emergent Strategy: Shaping Change, Changing Worlds by adrienne maree brown

RECOMMENDED READING

This Is Not A Drill: An Extinction Rebellion Handbook

A Better Planet: Forty Big Ideas for a Sustainable Future by Daniel C. Esty

The Great Derangement by Amitav Ghosh

Writing Ecofiction: Navigating the Challenges of Environmental Narrative by Kevan Manwaring

We all die at the end: Storytelling in the Climate Apocalypse by Sam Haddow

How to Fall in Love with the Future: A Time Traveller's Guide to Changing the World by Rob Hopkins

Doughnut Economics by Kate Raworth

Degrowth by Jason Hickel

You are what your Food Ate by David Montgomery and Anne Bicklé

How Minds Change by David McRaney

Supercommunicators by Charles Duhigg

High Conflict by Amanda Ripley

Post Work by Helen Hester and Will Strong

Feeding Each Other by Nicole Civita and Michelle Auerbach

Beastly: A New History of Animals and Us by Keggie Carew

Sacred Nature: How we can recover our bond with the natural world by Karen Armstrong

Undrowned: Black Feminist Lessons from Marine Mammals by Alexis Pauline Gumbs

Tending Grief: Embodied Rituals for Holding Our Sorrow and Growing Cultures of Care in Community by Camille Barton

Hothouse Earth: An Inhabitant's Guide by Bill McGuire

 # BOOKS TO READ

TITLE	AUTHOR

TITLE   DATE

AUTHOR

THOUGHTS

☆ ☆ ☆ ☆ ☆   CLIMATE
                              SOLUTIONS
                              INCLUDED?

TITLE   DATE

AUTHOR

THOUGHTS

☆ ☆ ☆ ☆ ☆   CLIMATE
                              SOLUTIONS
                              INCLUDED?

TITLE   DATE

AUTHOR

THOUGHTS

☆ ☆ ☆ ☆ ☆   CLIMATE
                    SOLUTIONS
                    INCLUDED? ◯

TITLE   DATE

AUTHOR

THOUGHTS

☆ ☆ ☆ ☆ ☆   CLIMATE
                    SOLUTIONS
                    INCLUDED? ◯

READING LIST

TITLE   DATE

AUTHOR

THOUGHTS

☆ ☆ ☆ ☆ ☆   CLIMATE
                   SOLUTIONS
                   INCLUDED? ◯

TITLE   DATE

AUTHOR

THOUGHTS

☆ ☆ ☆ ☆ ☆   CLIMATE
                   SOLUTIONS
                   INCLUDED? ◯

TITLE	DATE
AUTHOR	
THOUGHTS	

☆ ☆ ☆ ☆ ☆   CLIMATE
                      SOLUTIONS ◯
                      INCLUDED?

TITLE	DATE
AUTHOR	
THOUGHTS	

☆ ☆ ☆ ☆ ☆   CLIMATE
                      SOLUTIONS ◯
                      INCLUDED?

TITLE   DATE

AUTHOR

THOUGHTS

☆ ☆ ☆ ☆ ☆   CLIMATE
                      SOLUTIONS
                      INCLUDED?   ◯

TITLE   DATE

AUTHOR

THOUGHTS

☆ ☆ ☆ ☆ ☆   CLIMATE
                      SOLUTIONS
                      INCLUDED?   ◯

RESEARCH NOTES

RESEARCH NOTES

RESEARCH NOTES

WRITING MEMENTOS

Stick in receipts from coffeeshop writing sessions, print-outs covered in scribbles, or ideas jotted on the back of napkins!

WRITING MEMENTOS

WRITING MEMENTOS

EMOTION TRACKER

HOW I FELT BEFORE WRITING

HOW I FELT AFTER WRITING

HOW MY CHARACTERS FEEL

HOW I WANT MY READERS TO FEEL

POSITIVE FEEDBACK RECEIVED

CONSTRUCTIVE FEEDBACK RECEIVED

THINGS TO ADJUST
WHEN EDITING

THINGS TO ADJUST
WHEN EDITING

PITCHING YOUR PROJECT

You've finished your project! Congratulations! Now let's get it out to readers. Here are some tips for querying agents and pitching to publishers.

STEP 1: Find your unique selling points

Think about what makes you and your project special. Do you have a unique perspective or life experiences? Are you writing something with a good 'hook' that would make a reader yell 'TAKE MY MONEY!' if they saw the description in a bookshop?

Look at recent book deal announcements in publishing news outlets (e.g. Publishers Weekly, The Bookseller). What buzzwords are being used to describe books? This could be: *unreliable narrator, magical realism, dark academia, twisty, speculative/high concept, character-focused.*

MY BUZZWORDS

These pages are based on the 'Building a Bestseller' workshop by Wren James
wrenjames.co.uk/school-visits/

STEP 2: Create a Tagline

Use your buzzwords to create a short description of your project. For example, "A girl alone on a spaceship finds a connection with another ship, just at the time she needs it most" (The Loneliest Girl in the Universe) or "A teen romance between an ordinary girl and a boy who is actually a vampire" (Twilight).

This should be two sentences at most. Highlight what is most appealing about your project. As a reader, what is most memorable for you? How would you describe it to a friend to get them to read it?

[Character] must [do something] to [achieve story goal] or else [stakes if it fails].

MY TAGLINE

STEP 3: Create a longer outline

Describe the plot and themes of your project. Show off your best material - convince people the full text is worth reading (for pitching to agents and publishers, you might even want to spoil your plot twists!)

Include key details like:

- Who is your main character? Is there an ensemble group?
- What journey are you taking your characters on?
- What is the plot – is it emotion- or action-focussed?
- What is going to draw your reader in?
- What have you done differently from other books?
- Where is the setting, in time and place?
- What is the writing style – is it modern, pacey or descriptive? It is in a first person character-focussed perspective or more expansive and broad, jumping around the world and multiple people?
- What is the conflict? What dilemmas do the characters face?
- How do the stakes increase as time goes on? How do new events build on what has happened before?
- What is the character's emotional arc, and how do they change by the end? What are the key relationships?
- How have you woven climate themes into the story?

STEP 4: Personal biography

Write your own biography. Who are you, in demographic terms? Why are you the right person to tell this story?
- For example, are you a police officer writing a crime novel or a PhD History student writing a historical novel?

Include any previous publishing history, writing competitions or mentoring programmes you've participated in. Show you've invested in improving your writing craft, and have knowledge of the publishing industry.

Mention if you use social media to engage in publishing-related discussions, such as posting book reviews on 'bookstagram'. Talk about your passion for climate-focussed fiction!

STEP 5: Assemble a submission list

Look for literary agents and publishers who are open to submissions, who have expressed an interest in projects like yours. Some resources:

- The Climate Fiction Writers League database (climate-fiction.org/literary-agent-database)
- Manuscript Wishlist (manuscriptwishlist.com / mswishlist.com)
- Query Tracker (querytracker.net)
- The Writers and Artists Yearbook

Here's a template you can use to assemble your query letter:

Dear _____,

I'm writing to seek representation for [TITLE], a [GENRE/FORMAT] book of [115,000] words.

[SHORT TAGLINE].

I saw on your website that you are interested in _____, which my project includes. My novel is [A WELL-KNOWN BOOK] meets [A WELL-KNOWN MOVIE].

The book is about [LONGER OUTLINE].

I am passionate about weaving solutions-focused, uplifting climate themes into my work. In particular, this project features _____.

I am a [BIOGRAPHY]. I've undertaken [WRITING COURSES/WORKSHOPS] to help me edit my work.

I enclose the first three chapters and a synopsis, as requested on your website. I look forward to hearing from you. Thank you for your time.

Please follow the guidelines given on literary agents and publishers' websites when submitting your work. Be aware there are many scammers out there - you shouldn't need to pay to submit your work.

- Only submit to a few people at a time, so you can adjust your project based on new feedback
- Follow up <u>once</u> after a minimum of six weeks
- If they reject your submission, you can politely ask for feedback. Thank them for their time!
- Do not chase feedback
- Do not call or DM them on social media
- Remember that they will get a lot of submissions. A lack of reply is not personal or connected to your book.

Things to double-check before hitting send, alongside spelling and grammar:

- Have you given enough context to understand the writing sample? Is your sample setting up the rest of the project?
- Does your sample showcase your distinctive voice?
- Read your dialogue aloud - is it realistic or clunky? Can you follow the thread of the conversations?
- Are the stakes/goals/messages clear?
- Are you including too much info-dumping or exposition?
- Is your climate messaging too preachy, depressing or politically charged?

PUBLICATION CHECKLIST

When considering a publisher for your project, here are some questions you might want to ask them:

1. Have you signed up to a Publishers Association pledge on climate action, or do you have an alternative reduction strategy?

2. Have you set emissions targets with the Science Based Targets initiative (SBTi), the global standard? Have you set a net zero goal?

3. Do you disclose your carbon emissions annually to the Carbon Disclosure Project (CDP), and/or are you reporting in other ways?

4. Do you use 100% renewable electricity across your operations?

5. Do you plan to use 100% recycled paper, or otherwise sustainably source the paper used for packaging, books (where possible) and across your operations? Have you stopped using plastic packaging?

6. Have you taken specific action to protect biodiversity, limit deforestation and reduce water usage?

7. Do you use foils and finishes or lamination? What proportion of these can be recycled? Do you offer more sustainable formats such as trimmed sizes?

8. Does your organisation have a corporate governance system to hold it accountable for sustainability? Do you provide staff sustainability training?

9. Do you disclose any of your organisation's investments (including employees' pensions) in the fossil fuel industry?

10. How can you help me communicate this information prominently to my readers?

Authors want to feel proud of our books – not only our words and artwork, but also the physical volumes. By asking questions like this, we can help ensure our work is printed and distributed sustainably by a publisher committed to net-zero targets.

 These questions were developed with the Society of Authors.
societyofauthors.org/TreeToMe

UPCOMING EVENTS

Make a note of any future courses, panels, conventions, or submission deadlines which you'd like to participate in (or ideas for events you could run yourself!)

MONTH	MON	TUE	WED
○ JAN			
○ FEB			
○ MAR			
○ APR			
○ MAY			
○ JUN			
○ JUL			
○ AUG			
○ SEP			
○ OCT			
○ NOV			
○ DEC			

THU	FRI	SAT	SUN

MONTH	MON	TUE	WED
○ JAN			
○ FEB			
○ MAR			
○ APR			
○ MAY			
○ JUN			
○ JUL			
○ AUG			
○ SEP			
○ OCT			
○ NOV			
○ DEC			

THU	FRI	SAT	SUN

MONTH	MON	TUE	WED
○ JAN			
○ FEB			
○ MAR			
○ APR			
○ MAY			
○ JUN			
○ JUL			
○ AUG			
○ SEP			
○ OCT			
○ NOV			
○ DEC			

THU	FRI	SAT	SUN

MONTH	MON	TUE	WED
○ JAN			
○ FEB			
○ MAR			
○ APR			
○ MAY			
○ JUN			
○ JUL			
○ AUG			
○ SEP			
○ OCT			
○ NOV			
○ DEC			

THU	FRI	SAT	SUN

MONTH	MON	TUE	WED
○ JAN			
○ FEB			
○ MAR			
○ APR			
○ MAY			
○ JUN			
○ JUL			
○ AUG			
○ SEP			
○ OCT			
○ NOV			
○ DEC			

THU	FRI	SAT	SUN

MONTH	MON	TUE	WED
○ JAN			
○ FEB			
○ MAR			
○ APR			
○ MAY			
○ JUN			
○ JUL			
○ AUG			
○ SEP			
○ OCT			
○ NOV			
○ DEC			

THU	FRI	SAT	SUN

MONTHLY WRITING HABIT TRACKER

Each segment represents a day of the month. Colour in squares to track your writing that day.

JAN FEB MAR APR MAY JUN JUL AUG SEP OCT NOV DEC

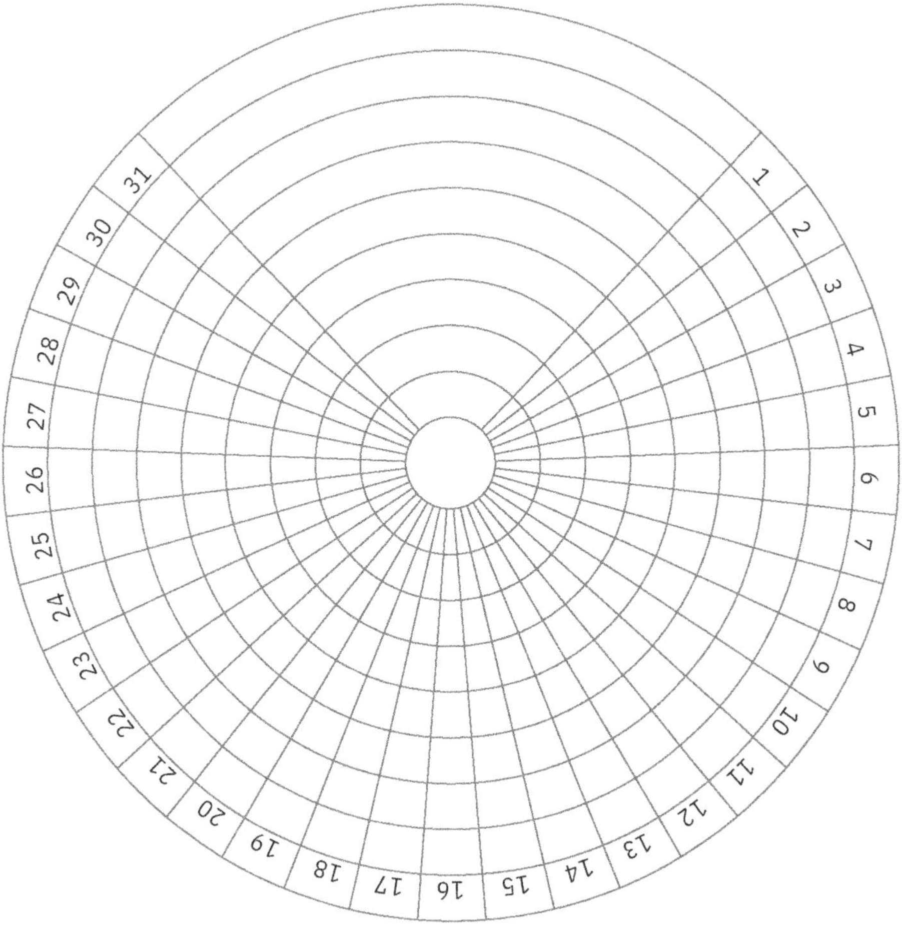

TOTAL MONTHLY WORD COUNT:

MONTHLY WRITING HABIT TRACKER

Each segment represents a day of the month. Colour in squares to track your writing that day.

JAN FEB MAR APR MAY JUN JUL AUG SEP OCT NOV DEC

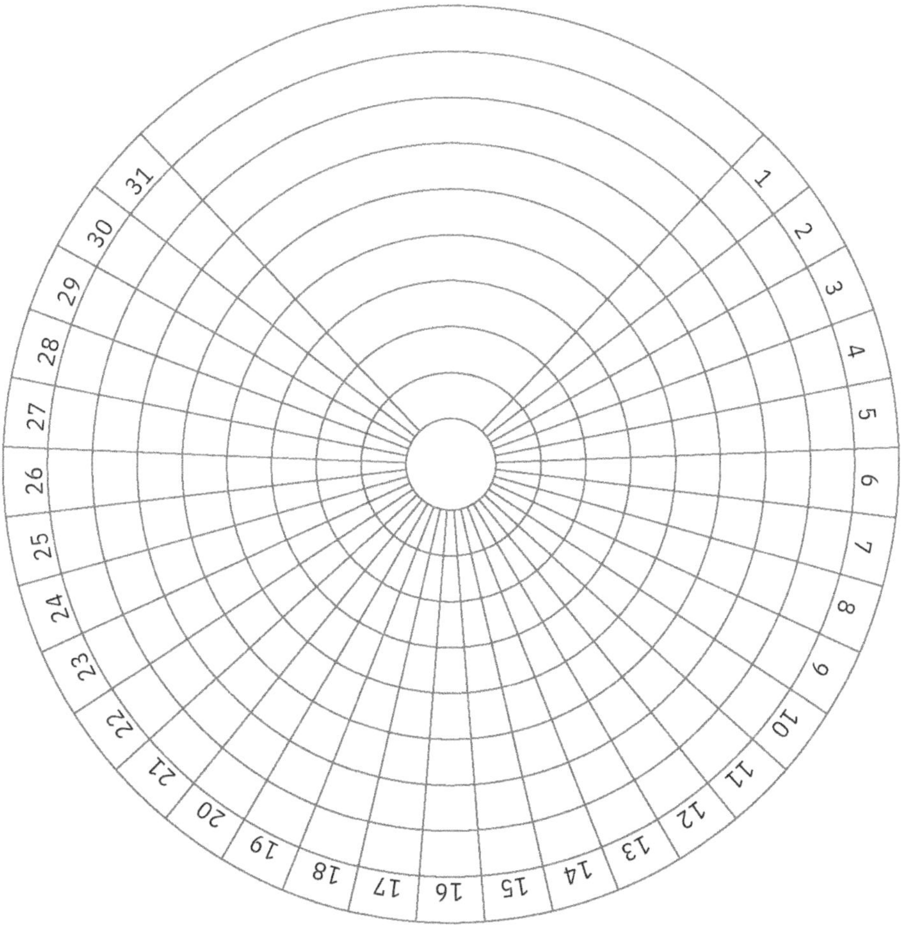

TOTAL MONTHLY WORD COUNT:

MONTHLY WRITING HABIT TRACKER

Each segment represents a day of the month. Colour in squares to track your writing that day.

JAN FEB MAR APR MAY JUN JUL AUG SEP OCT NOV DEC

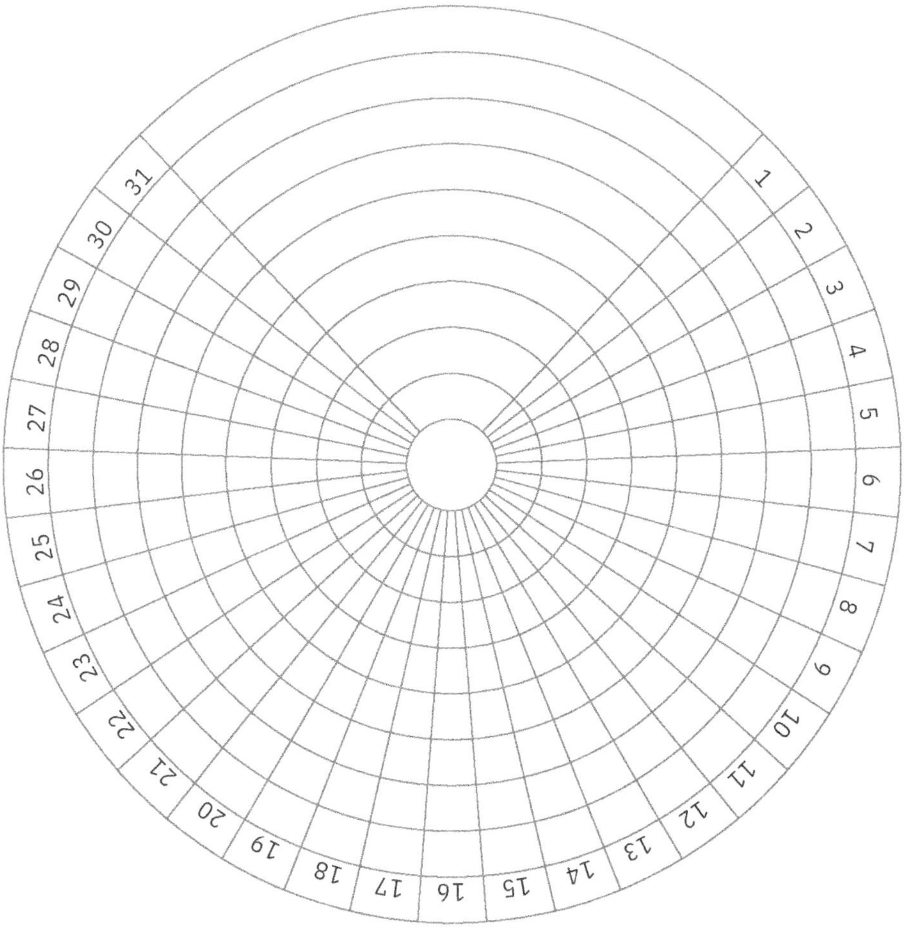

TOTAL MONTHLY WORD COUNT:

MONTHLY WRITING
HABIT TRACKER

Each segment represents a day of the month. Colour in squares to track your writing that day.

JAN FEB MAR APR MAY JUN JUL AUG SEP OCT NOV DEC

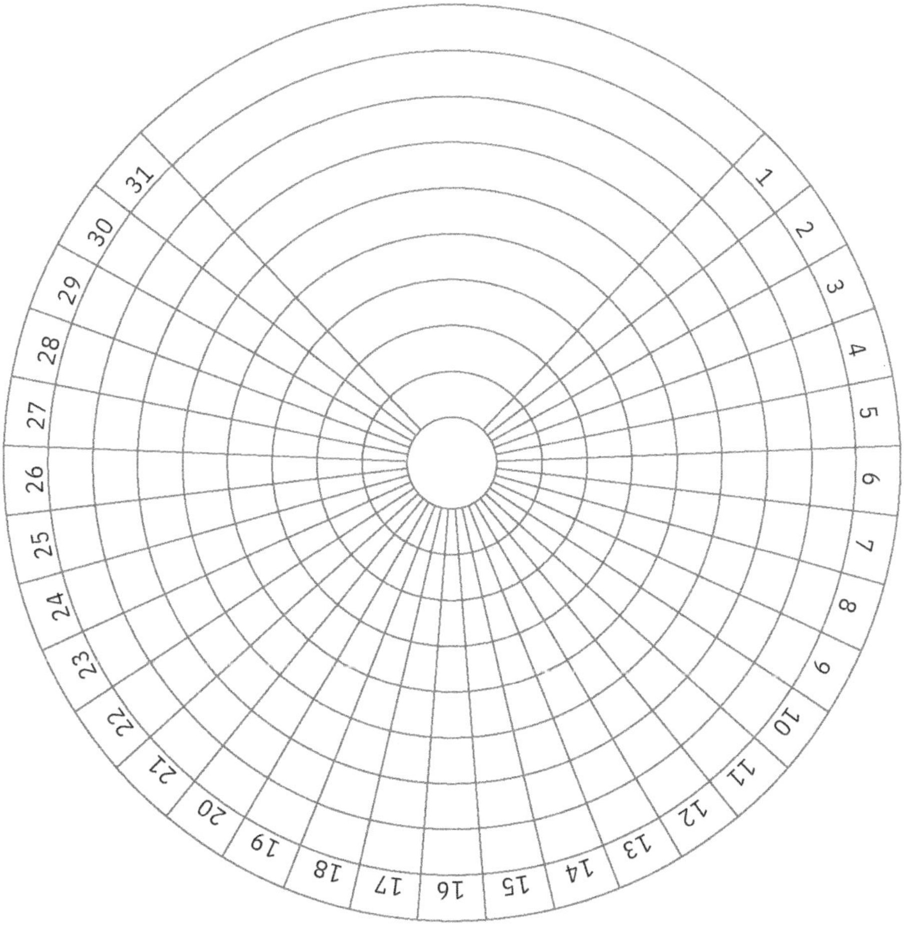

TOTAL MONTHLY WORD COUNT:

MONTHLY WRITING HABIT TRACKER

Each segment represents a day of the month. Colour in squares to track your writing that day.

JAN FEB MAR APR MAY JUN JUL AUG SEP OCT NOV DEC

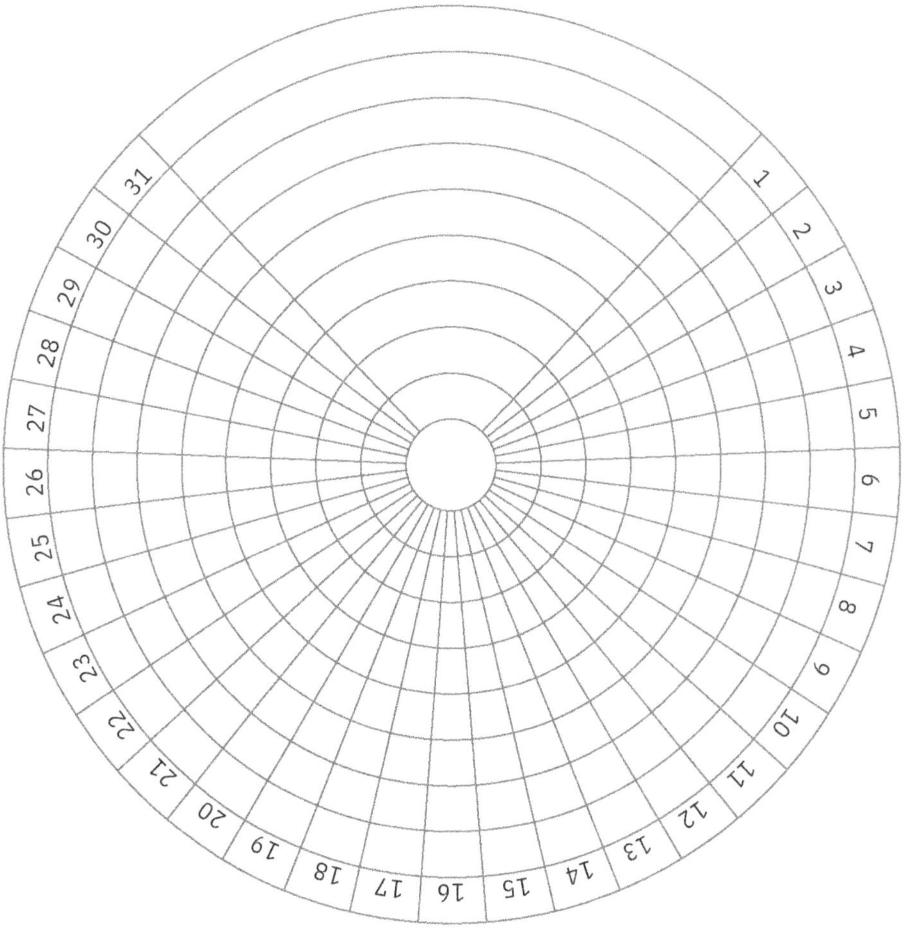

TOTAL MONTHLY WORD COUNT:

MONTHLY WRITING HABIT TRACKER

Each segment represents a day of the month. Colour in squares to track your writing that day.

JAN FEB MAR APR MAY JUN JUL AUG SEP OCT NOV DEC

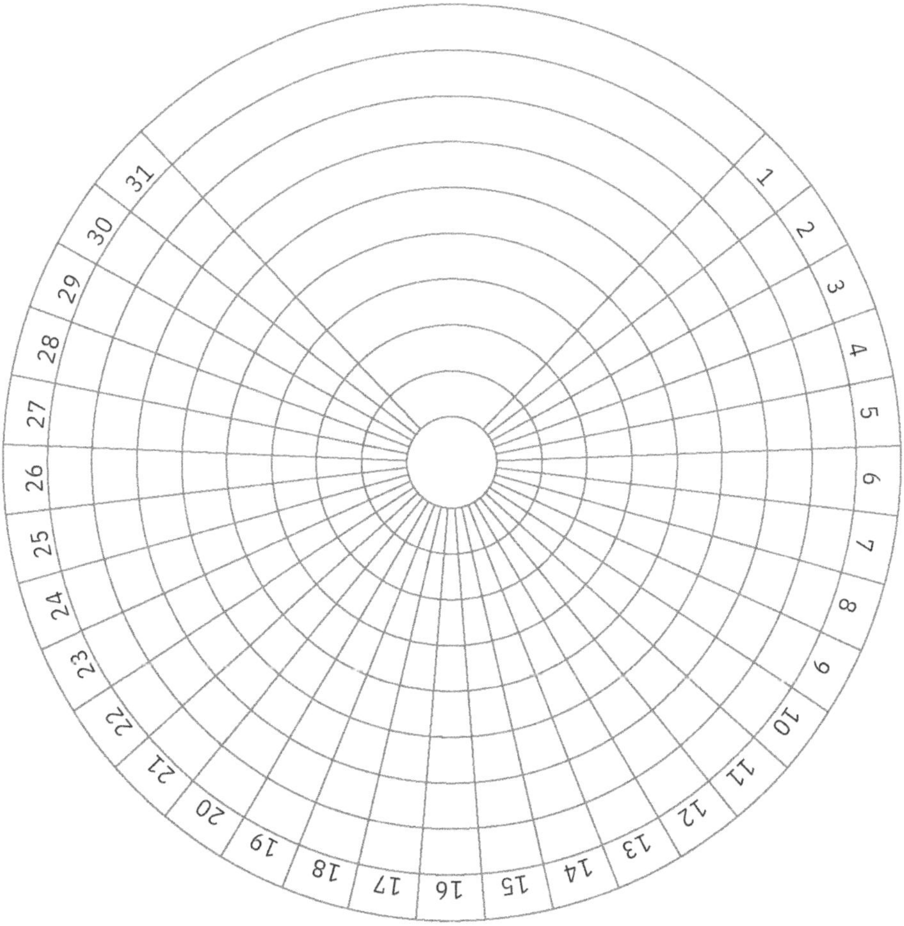

TOTAL MONTHLY WORD COUNT:

WEEKLY PLANNER

MONDAY

TUESDAY

WEDNESDAY

THURSDAY

FRIDAY

SATURDAY

SUNDAY

NOTES:

_____

_____

_____

_____

WEEKLY PLANNER

MONDAY	**TUESDAY**
WEDNESDAY	**THURSDAY**
FRIDAY	**SATURDAY**
SUNDAY	**NOTES:**

WEEKLY PLANNER

MONDAY	**TUESDAY**
WEDNESDAY	**THURSDAY**
FRIDAY	**SATURDAY**
SUNDAY	**NOTES:**

_____
_____
_____
_____

WEEKLY PLANNER

MONDAY	TUESDAY
WEDNESDAY	**THURSDAY**
FRIDAY	**SATURDAY**
SUNDAY	**NOTES:**

WEEKLY PLANNER

MONDAY

TUESDAY

WEDNESDAY

THURSDAY

FRIDAY

SATURDAY

SUNDAY

NOTES:

_____

_____

_____

_____

WEEKLY PLANNER

MONDAY	TUESDAY
WEDNESDAY	THURSDAY
FRIDAY	SATURDAY
SUNDAY	NOTES:

NOTES:

_____

_____

_____

_____

WEEKLY PLANNER

MONDAY	TUESDAY
WEDNESDAY	**THURSDAY**
FRIDAY	**SATURDAY**
SUNDAY	**NOTES:**

WEEKLY PLANNER

MONDAY

TUESDAY

WEDNESDAY

THURSDAY

FRIDAY

SATURDAY

SUNDAY

NOTES:

_____

_____

_____

_____

WEEKLY PLANNER

MONDAY	TUESDAY
WEDNESDAY	**THURSDAY**
FRIDAY	**SATURDAY**
SUNDAY	**NOTES:**

WEEKLY PLANNER

MONDAY	TUESDAY
WEDNESDAY	**THURSDAY**
FRIDAY	**SATURDAY**
SUNDAY	**NOTES:**

WEEKLY PLANNER

MONDAY	TUESDAY
WEDNESDAY	**THURSDAY**
FRIDAY	**SATURDAY**
SUNDAY	**NOTES:** _____ _____ _____ _____

WEEKLY PLANNER

MONDAY	TUESDAY
WEDNESDAY	**THURSDAY**
FRIDAY	**SATURDAY**
SUNDAY	**NOTES:**

WEEKLY PLANNER

MONDAY

TUESDAY

WEDNESDAY

THURSDAY

FRIDAY

SATURDAY

SUNDAY

NOTES:

_____

_____

_____

_____

WEEKLY PLANNER

MONDAY	TUESDAY
WEDNESDAY	THURSDAY
FRIDAY	SATURDAY
SUNDAY	NOTES:

NOTES:

_____

_____

_____

_____

WEEKLY PLANNER

MONDAY

TUESDAY

WEDNESDAY

THURSDAY

FRIDAY

SATURDAY

SUNDAY

NOTES:

_____

_____

_____

_____

WEEKLY PLANNER

MONDAY

TUESDAY

WEDNESDAY

THURSDAY

FRIDAY

SATURDAY

SUNDAY

NOTES:

_____

_____

_____

_____

WEEKLY PLANNER

MONDAY	TUESDAY

WEDNESDAY	THURSDAY

FRIDAY	SATURDAY

SUNDAY

NOTES:

_____

_____

_____

_____

WEEKLY PLANNER

MONDAY	TUESDAY

WEDNESDAY	THURSDAY

FRIDAY	SATURDAY

SUNDAY	NOTES:
	_____
	_____
	_____
	_____

WEEKLY PLANNER

MONDAY	TUESDAY
WEDNESDAY	**THURSDAY**
FRIDAY	**SATURDAY**
SUNDAY	**NOTES:**

NOTES:

_____
_____
_____
_____

WEEKLY PLANNER

MONDAY

TUESDAY

WEDNESDAY

THURSDAY

FRIDAY

SATURDAY

SUNDAY

NOTES:

_____

_____

_____

_____

WEEKLY PLANNER

MONDAY	TUESDAY
WEDNESDAY	**THURSDAY**
FRIDAY	**SATURDAY**
SUNDAY	**NOTES:**

WEEKLY PLANNER

MONDAY

TUESDAY

WEDNESDAY

THURSDAY

FRIDAY

SATURDAY

SUNDAY

NOTES:

_____
_____
_____
_____

WEEKLY PLANNER

MONDAY

TUESDAY

WEDNESDAY

THURSDAY

FRIDAY

SATURDAY

SUNDAY

NOTES:

_____

_____

_____

_____

WEEKLY PLANNER

MONDAY

TUESDAY

WEDNESDAY

THURSDAY

FRIDAY

SATURDAY

SUNDAY

NOTES:

_____

_____

_____

_____

WEEKLY PLANNER

MONDAY	TUESDAY

WEDNESDAY	THURSDAY

FRIDAY	SATURDAY

SUNDAY	NOTES:
	_____
	_____
	_____
	_____

WEEKLY PLANNER

MONDAY

TUESDAY

WEDNESDAY

THURSDAY

FRIDAY

SATURDAY

SUNDAY

NOTES:

_____

_____

_____

_____

HUMAN MINDS RELY ON
STORIES AS THE
PRIMARY ROADMAP FOR
UNDERSTANDING,
MAKING SENSE OF,
REMEMBERING, AND
PLANNING OUR LIVES.
WE THINK IN STORY
TERMS.

KENDALL HAVEN

This work is dedicated to the memory of League members Nicky Singer and Marcus Sedgwick.

Journal created by Wren James, founder of the Climate Fiction Writers League

climate-fiction.org   wrenjames.co.uk
@climatefictionwritersleague @wrenjameswriter

You are welcome to photocopy the pages of this handbook to use in workshops or teaching. Please just include a credit line on each page. However, do not digitalise this book or use it to train generative AI.

Book cover design by Rosemary Linnell (@rtlinnell)
Logo design by Douwe van Schie

2025

With thanks to Climate Spring, Rewriting Earth, Green Stories, the Society of Authors and their Sustainability Network Steering Committee, Heard, and the Center for Science and the Imagination; as well as Lucy Stone, Claire Wilson, Rachel James, Rosemary Linnell, Kevan Manwaring, Sam Haddow, Jessica Miles, Eva Svenstedt Ward, Manda Scott, Steve Willis, Emily Coren, Denise Baden, Paul Goodenough, Ian Edwards, James Stewart, K Roméy, Mrs Frollein, J. L. Westover, Joel Pett, Joan Chan, Laura Baggaley, Ilse Pedler, Katherine Stansfield, Hilary Watson, Alice Willitts, Joey Eschrich, Zino Akaka, Andrew Hudson and Maggie Behling.

For a 20% discount on membership to the Society of Authors, use code **mship2025** at societyofauthors.org

Printed in Dunstable, United Kingdom